Me and My Father's Shadow

A Daughter's Quest and Biography

Of

Ted Lewis "The Jazz King"

Me and My Father's Shadow

A Daughter's Quest and Biography
of
Ted Lewis "The Jazz King"

Dawn Williams

SUNRISE HOUSE
Publishers

ME AND MY FATHER'S SHADOW
A Daughter's Quest and Biography
of
Ted Lewis "The Jazz King"

Cover and Book Design by
Scott Willis

Publishers

ISBN 0-9770783-1-0

Published by
Sunrise House Publishers
P.O. Box 327
Seal Beach, CA 90740

PRINTED IN THE UNITED STATES OF AMERICA

Praise for
ME AND MY FATHER'S SHADOW
A Daughter's Quest and Biography
of
Ted Lewis "The Jazz King"

"Detective story, history, memoir and biography - Dawn Williams' investigation into the life of Ted Lewis soars above those categories to establish its own unique and affecting genre. Memorable."
> - A.J. Languth, author of "Our Vietnam" and "Saki: A Life of Hector Munro."

"Dawn Williams is an amazing woman who has written a remarkable book about her real father, the legendary band-leading icon, Ted Lewis."
> - Gene Corman, producer of the Emmy-winning mini-series "Golda," which starred Ingrid Begman.

"Dawn Williams has written a great book that I couldn't put down."
> - Ellen Lively Steele, Former New Mexico State Senator, 1984-1988.

"From a very personal advantage, Dawn Williams has provided a look into the colorful past of Ted Lewis in this biography that answers many questions before unanswered about his life."
> - Doris Wenzel, author and editor, Mayhaven Publishing.

"Me and My Father's Shadow finally sheds light on one of our industry's most prolific recording artists and actors. A man who was loved by all, a personal friend of our family, and who'll now be immortalized by his daughter in this highly entertaining and factual book."
> - Chris Costello and Paddy Costello Humphreys, daughters of Lou Costello (Abbot and Costello).

Dedication

To each of my four children

Dana
Kenny
Larry
Linda

"The jewels in my crown"

and to my wonderful
grandchildren

Author's Note

Although this is a work of non-fiction, some portions of the content are fictionalized, since the alternative - not including them at all - would have detracted from the overall truth of the story:

- Some anecdotal narrations and dialogue are reconstructions or speculations.

- In the interest of privacy and anonymity, pseudonyms are used for persons whose names are not biographically significant. Names of Ted Lewis' relatives and of public officials and celebrities are accurately recounted.

- *The Lonedale Operator*, an early silent film, could not be located. The scene of the daughter praying at her father's bedside is generic, based on similar scenes filmed for other silent movies.

- It could not be confimed that Al Jolson sang *Danny Boy* in the burlesque theater.

The reader will encounter a number of racial and ethnic references that are currently disfavored yet were acceptable at the time; these were left unchanged because they are a part of history.

Chapter titles are generally Ted Lewis song titles. *When the Moon Comes Over the Mountain* is an exception; that was Kate Smith's theme song.

Although the author believes that Ted Lewis is her biological father, no legal action has ever been taken to establish this. In any event, this book's intended focus is not on the author but on the subject, and what it was actually like to see in person a Ted Lewis stage performance. As a personal memoir, *Me and My Father's Shadow* is a primary source regarding the life of Ted Lewis, a famous and beloved entertainment icon, and an important part of the history of jazz. It is hoped that the reader will come away with a renewed appreciation for the various categories of jazz and their role in the evolution of American music through the late 1800s, through the 1900s, and of course, for the inimitable Ted Lewis, "The Jazz King."

- Dawn Williams

Introduction

Indianapolis, Indiana: Sunday afternoon, 1948

The gargantuan red velvet curtain was trimmed in gold brocade, and stretched across the entire stage of the Circle Theater. I was 13 years old, and it seemed to me at least 50 feet across. Its size alone was an icon of great entertainment.

The Circle was a premier movie house of downtown Indianapolis located on famous Monument Circle. It projected first run movies, featured "Big Bands," and today, live on stage, was my favorite bandleader and entertainer, Ted Lewis, whom I never missed seeing when he came to Indianapolis. Even winter's inclement weather with its snow or icy roads could not keep me away.

"When my baby smiles at me..." sang a voice accompanied by an orchestra, both vocalist and band hidden by this curtain that now parted and shimmered as the gold brocade undulated like wheat bobbing in a wind-swept field. As if by magic, a band of about 50 musicians appeared, barely visible through a haze of gauze screen, the song grew louder, and the singer appeared from the theater wing as he strolled onto its stage.

There he was. Ted Lewis singing his theme song, When My Baby Smiles At Me, as he stepped into full view of the audience, dressed in his black tuxedo with a carnation in his lapel, his smart, black cane under his arm. This was the diminutive musician/vocalist/entertainer/ band leader who, with a tap of his finger adjusted his battered top hat, then so proudly strutted across the stage with the last words of his song, "...It's just a bit of Heaven when My baby Smiles at me...."

The audience went wild. They howled, clapped, and cheered. As a small town Hoosier boy, this was music to die for that day as my ears were filled with other Ted Lewis songs such as, "She's Funny That Way" and "Me and My Shadow." I'd seen other band leaders at the Circle...Carmen Cavallero, Freddy Martin, Henry Busse...but Mr. Lewis was a class act. Each one of us there that day was getting what we came to see: Ted Lewis, our undisputed icon of entertainment, and reigning "Jazz King" of the world. He was "The Best of the Best."

By Wayne Kelly: Los Angeles Times Director of Photography and Picture Editor

Table of Contents

Book One : *Dawn*

Book Two : *Ted*

Book Three : *Circleville* *Capital of the World*

Prologue

"Glad Rag Doll"

Los Angeles, June, 1928

The young matron knew she was attractive, almost beautiful, an image confirmed by her reflection as she adjusted the rear view mirror above the windshield of her practically new green Packard touring car.

"Swell," she said, smiling at what she saw. Taking her hand off the mirror, her fingers tucked into place renegade wisps of short auburn-brown hair peeking out from under her black velvet cloche. She bought the *chapeau* - "That means *hat* in French, you know" - the salesgirl at Bullocks said yesterday, especially for tonight. Now she made sure it framed her face at just the right coquettish angle. *He'll love it*, she thought, and started to hum his theme song.

Confident, *and a little wicked*, a self-rebuke she quickly abandoned as she drove west on Wilshire Boulevard toward their *rendezvous*, she giggled at using her high school French. As if she were not alone and others in the car were scowling at her boldness. But, she was enjoying the excitement of mystery and intrigue, and she banished the imaginary passengers from her mind.

She had wanted to be alone with him for a long time,

i

and she knew exactly what was going to happen, ignoring any possible consequences. Tonight she would sweep into tomorrow her concerns for today. Besides, she told herself, she had an excuse. Hadn't Fred told her to call him? He even suggested that she meet him and his wife after the show at the Palace Theater. Fred was probably feeling a little guilty about going on his three-month long business trip without her.

At first, she felt hurt when he told her he was going alone. Since their marriage, they always went together. Traveling to the East Coast where Fred planned the studies for several colleges and universities was the most exciting part of being Mrs. Fred Whipple. She even liked being thirty-six years younger than he was, enjoying her role as his "glorious little girl" who was often mistaken as the daughter of her distinguished looking husband. Impeccably dressed, generous with money, affection and consideration, Fred was her ideal of a true aristocrat. She felt comfortable, secure in knowing she had married well. Head-over-heels in love, she often thought, could wait.

The very best part, however, was actually seeing cities that once were only names. New York. Boston. Chicago. *If we hadn't been in New York where he and his band were playing at Rector's, I might never have met him.* She remembered how thrilled she was when Fred took her to dinner at the famous nightclub and introduced her during intermission to his long-time friend. After his show, joined by his wife, they all went to another nightclub for drinks and dancing. *Me. He danced with me.* She remembered that sudden sharp excitement throughout her body at that moment when he took her in his arms and twirled her about the floor.

While Fred was away, he certainly wanted his very young wife to have fun, she thought. "Why not see the Palace show where he and his orchestra are playing?" Fred said. "Even have dinner with them afterward." Fred's suggestion was typical. So thoughtful. *He just wanted me to have something to look forward to while he was gone.*

When she heard his wife would not be able to join them, at first she was sorry. Now, tonight it would be just the two of them. She remembered him saying that and she smiled.

The late hour, almost midnight, left Wilshire Boulevard empty of its usual traffic. Only an occasional car passed her. Grateful for the deserted boulevard, she could focus on finding her destination: The Ambassador Hotel.

Since it opened seven years ago on New Years Day, the Ambassador sprawled like a giant letter **H** over 160 acres of pastoral wheat land that provided shelter for the world's royal, rich, and famous. Well, I'm not royal or rich, she thought, but he certainly is one of the most famous men in the world. He was famous enough for both of them.

"I'm here," she said aloud, thrilled and excited to see the dome-shaped crown of the Brown Derby restaurant across from the hotel. Guiding her Packard into the left-hand lane, she turned and drove to the hotel entrance. Awed by the Ambassador's glamour, she slowed and let the car glide onto the entrance drive, past lush landscape and toward the late-hour lights still glowing from a few hotel windows. In one of these rooms he would be waiting for her.

Ever since she left the Palace after his show tonight, she was imagining just what would happen when she arrived at the Ambassador. After the valet parked her car, she would walk through the lobby and do just as he had told her on the phone this morning. She would go directly to the room that a friend lent him for the evening. Gently, but firmly, she would knock, he would open the door, she would smile. Then taking her hand, he would put his arm about her waist and say, " My dear, I have been waiting so long for this moment." Guiding her into the room, he would kiss her sweetly, softly on her cheek, and whisper her name. Then, oh, so quietly, he would close the door behind them.

The sun is an early riser in June. Its soft morning light

flowed into the room as he walked with her to the door and kissed her, their lips reluctant to part and say good-by. When he closed the door behind her, the life she had known only the night before had changed forever.

Book One

Dawn

Chapter One

"A Jazz Holiday"

The Los Angeles Railway Company yellow streetcar rolled down Figueroa Street.

With one hand, standing passengers clung to black leather straps, as the streetcar swayed - *right* then *left* - just below Mount Washington, where the Southwest Museum paid Southern California's 1930's homage to its remnant of American Indian culture.

It was Sunday afternoon, and many of these Angelenos were making a Sunday trip to the movies in downtown Los Angeles. My mother and I joined the crowd, boarding the streetcar at Figueroa and Avenue 52. This was the street where my mother, grandmother, and I shared, at a depression-high cost of twenty dollars a month, the southern half of a one-bedroom duplex in Highland Park. The town was squeezed between Glendale to the north, Pasadena to the east, and also by Eagle Rock which had one cautious claim to fame: a dubious shadowy spread-eagle form etched by centuries on a stone that rose high above ground level. The three of us had moved to Highland Park just before my fifth birthday. Both women were widowed within months of each other when I was three and still living in Hollywood where I was born. But, this particular Sunday mother and I were a twosome rather than a trio. My grandmother, uncharacteristically, had chosen to stay home.

Once aboard the car, mother found a seat and said, "Dawn, sit here."

Obediently, I did.

She added, "Don't forget. Give up your seat to someone older or less fortunate than you."

My mother made it a suggestion rather than a command. Motherhood had been life's afterthought for Ruth Olive Dean Whipple. She was from the flapper era, a free spirit with no agenda. Correcting her only child had been based on her passivity with which she dealt with both the conquerors and mothers of the world. During an era that favored firm discipline, she embraced non-confrontation, a code of *do nothing, say nothing.*

She would, however, issue occasional maternal wisdom: "Dawn, you don't have to love a man to marry him," and "Dawn, after you get married never, never let your husband see you without lipstick and combed hair." Those pretty well exhausted her meager store of advice. The first of these I immediately discarded as irrational; the second, I mentally filed under *makes sense.*

Today, nobody old or infirm got on the streetcar, and I, a healthy eight-year-old, could sit instead of stand all the way to Ninth and Broadway. Near that corner was the Orpheum Theater, our ultimate destination, featuring a movie and stage show.

Our Sunday streetcar journey was an encore of our Saturday outing. As secretary to the Parole Board for the Los Angeles County District Attorneys Office, my mother's work was Monday through Friday plus a half day on Saturday mornings. Usually I accompanied her that day. For three wonderful hours between 9 a.m. and noon, I lived in the adult world of justice and crime. Deputy District Attorneys were in and out of my mother's office continually. Uniformed Deputy Sheriffs were also frequent visitors, and on occasion I could go with my mother while she delivered papers to both departments and the upstairs jail. I was allowed to roam the building at will and sometimes had a nickel to spend for candy at the lobby newsstand.

Under Mother's tutelage, I became a typewriter artist. She taught me how to make troops of all black ink armed soldiers wearing boots and shouldering rifles while standing in regiment lines. First, I would type the dollar sign across the page in a single line. Typing quotation marks underneath each body, I would form two boots. The last symbol was a slash sign across each body for the rifle. Other regiments could be refined by creating dollar-sign bodies and quotation mark boots in black, then slash line rifles in red. Options for creating typewriter armies, it seemed, were endless.

During the 1930s, Buron Fitts was the Los Angeles County District Attorney and had hired my mother in 1932 despite her ignorance of both typing and shorthand. Those prerequisites she had considered unnecessary, promising she would learn them after she was employed. Recently widowed and penniless, she had no means to support a three-year-old daughter and a sixty-two-year-old mother. Faced with gargantuan unpaid bills left by her deceased husband, and a harsh economy, she lost her Point View home to foreclosure and put me in a Los Angeles orphanage until she could provide for her family.

"I had gone to Manual Arts High School in Los Angeles at the same time as Buron," my mother often explained when I was growing up, "and he gave me the job." Four months later, adult night school had taught her to take shorthand and to type. Why, I thought, would he give her a job she could not do?

The District Attorney offices occupied the entire sixth floor of the twelve-story high Hall of Justice, a cube shaped building of dismal gray on the corner of Broadway and Temple Street, one block above First Street where the actual downtown Los Angeles business and theater district begins. Sheriff Eugene Biscaluz and his county Sheriffs offices were in the basement, while prisoners were confined in jail cells on the top floor where the condemned men nudged heaven while battling hell.

During those ten years my mother worked in the Hall of Justice, I would learn first hand that crime does not pay unless employed fighting it. Occasionally I would see celebrities at office Christmas parties or in the halls, including the four elevator operators who would often transport me from floor-to-floor, and were destined to become the famous Ink Spots Quartet. It seemed to me there was no end to the stories hidden in this old building.

***

"Why didn't Grandma come with us?" I asked my mother, the streetcar now stopped at First Street, awaiting its final transport down Broadway towards Ninth.

"Oh, she just decided to stay home today," she said, smiled, and turned to look out the window. My mother's way of telling me not to ask more questions.

I knew, however, my grandmother would never willingly miss this particular Sunday movie-plus-vaudeville show at the Orpheum. Ted Lewis, world-renown bandleader and entertainer, was featured on stage in one of his occasional Los Angeles performances, an event we three planned weeks ahead to attend. Mother, Grandma, and I shared a passion for his shows. Today, when Ted Lewis would ask the audience, "Is everybody happy?" Grandma would not be there to answer, "Yes." I wondered why. Just yesterday she made sure that we three looked at my mother's slightly worn photo of Ted Lewis smiling from beneath an old and battered top hat. A picture she would not return to our family photo album until my mother explained, "You know, Dawn, I used to dance with Ted Lewis." As a dancer, Mother had studied with renown teacher, Ruth Saint Dennis, later touring in the chorus with Fanchon and Marco Wolfe, a brother and sister dance team famous for their shows and Hollywood dance studio. Later she joined Colonel Diamond, an eighty-year-old

5

ballroom dancer, in a vaudeville act billed as "Youth and Old Age." Assuming she also had danced professionally on stage with Ted Lewis, it always seemed logical to me that he would have given her this photograph with the inscription, *To Ruth with love, Ted Lewis.*

I always loved to hear my mother tell this story and was thrilled by this final personal message to her that made Ted Lewis seem like part of our home. I imagined him signing the picture, and then pretend he was singing his theme song, <u>When My Baby Smiles At Me</u>, to the three of us.

My favorite Ted Lewis song, however, was <u>Me and My Shadow</u>, and I insisted on performing it after family company dinners. Since I needed a "shadow," my best friend, Sally, who lived across the street, reluctantly agreed to play the role. Together, she and I had taken dancing lessons together in Los Angeles. During that time we were in a recital and performed a tap dance on stage at a small auditorium inside Bullocks department store. Part of our routine was to catch our freestanding canes after we executed each of several full circle turns. Sally would sometimes drop her cane when she turned, unable to make the turn in time to grasp the cane before it fell. Embarrassed, she abandoned dancing lessons and show business. I convinced her, however, to be my shadow when I explained, "All you have to do, Sally, is to follow me across the living room and to make the same movements that I do. You don't even have to sing." Agreeing to the role of Shadow "just this once," we dressed in our tap dance recital costumes, including top hats and canes, ready to perform.

Our audience, never more than six adult family and friends, sat on the couch and dining room chairs that were lined up along the far side of the living room facing the dining area. Our entrance was through a hall door, opening onto that part of the floor where both rooms met. Our stage was an imaginary line separating the two rooms.

I was both announcer and Ted Lewis. Sally, of course, was my shadow, and we would stand in the hall next to the open door awaiting our entrance. Grandma played the piano. As soon as the audience was absolutely quiet, I walked alone through the entrance and took center stage.

"Ladies and gentlemen," I began, as the announcer, and tipped my hat," welcome to this beautiful theater where you will see Ted Lewis and his helper in <u>Me and My Shadow</u>. I would bow, replace my hat, and run back into the hall where I waited for the applause to stop. After the audience was quiet, I waited another few seconds before I started singing the first line of the featured song as Grandma began her accompaniment.

"*Me and my shadow, strolling down the avenue,*" I would begin, Sally and I still hidden in the hall. After the second "*Me and my shadow,*" I would start slowly through the door, making sure my hand, which was imitating those famous Ted Lewis gestures, was the first part of me that the audience saw. By the time I had finished the next words, "*not a soul to tell our troubles to,*" both Sally and I had passed through the doorway and were on stage in full view of the audience.

My plan, I explained to Sally, was this: as soon as the audience could see us both, we would continue walking, in time with my singing, and facing the opposite wall where the ten feet of "stage" ended. She was to follow me, copying every move I made while I sang. Our goal was to reach the far end of the stage, at the wall, the exact moment I completed the final words of the song, both ending at the same time.

"*When it's twelve o'clock,*" I continued singing, waving my hand upwards in circular gestures, like Ted Lewis did, for "*we climb the stairs,*" ending with a two-beat, clenched-fist knock on an imaginary door as I sang, "*We never knock, 'cause nobody's there.*" Now well past the half-way point and approaching the end of our stage, Sally and I would turn to the audience, ending our performance and my song with those last words, "*Just me and my shadow, all alone and feeling blue."*

Applause rocked the living room. Sally bent slightly with
a hint of a bow. I bowed so low my hat fell to the floor. Picking
it up, I held it with both hands by its brim and bowed, one, two,
three times more, smiling at the audience and refusing to budge
from this fame and applause. Grandma always clapped the hardest
of anyone in the audience and was my greatest fan.

"You were a fine Ted Lewis," she said after our show,
hugging and kissing me. "Now, where did your shadow go?" and
she went looking for Sally to give her a hug and a kiss and tell her,
"Sally, you were the best shadow I ever saw."

I loved to perform whenever we had company at home
and often did other musical routines, or plays that I would make
up. But, Me and My Shadow was always everybody's favorite,
especially my grandmother's. Just as she would never have missed
one of my own Ted Lewis "shows," I knew she wanted to be with
us today to see the real Ted Lewis and his shadow walk across a
real stage at the Orpheum theater.

"I miss Grandma," I said to my mother as the yellow car
started up again from First Street, jolting those passengers who
had not found vacant seats and were still clinging to the leather
straps hanging from above.

"I know you do, Dawn." This time she kissed my cheek
before smiling and turning to look out the window.

Our streetcar now lumbered down Broadway and through
the Los Angeles business and theater district, preparing to stop
for passengers to get off at each corner of the numbered cross
streets as it rolled toward Ninth. First, we passed the Grand
Central Market, a mammoth grocery store that occupied a city
block. Here I could smell freshly ground peanut butter whenever
I watched the store clerk pack it into cartons as it oozed from
the grinder. Peanut brittle was made at a nearby candy store by
candy makers turning and folding the warm confection on a
marble slab in the store's front window. Mechanical animated

Christmas displays drew thousands each season to Bullocks and The Broadway department stores' display windows. Clifton's Cafeteria, where I had my fourth birthday party, and The Pig 'n Whistle were favorite places to eat when Mother could afford it. Finally, when I saw its sea-green tower rising high above the Eastern Columbia building across the street from the Orpheum, I knew we were almost at our destination.

"Mommy, hurry," I said, jumping out of my seat before the streetcar came to a full stop. I grabbed her hand, urged her from the wooden seat, and pulled her toward the car's exit.

"What's your hurry?" she said, and giggled as if not expecting an answer. Then Mother followed me, stopping briefly on the final step and looking towards the theater. For a moment I thought she looked sad, but she smiled again and said, "All right, Dawn, let's go to the show." She took my hand and we walked toward the Orpheum, our eyes glued to the theater marquee ahead that read:

TED LEWIS   LIVE ON STAGE

Chapter Two

"On The Sunny Side of the Street"

After we left the streetcar, Mother and I stepped directly into a safety zone provided for passengers in the middle of the street next to the streetcar.

"Take my hand, Dawn," she said, and pulled me close to her. "Let's wait for the signal to change before we cross the street."

I looked toward the signal posts at Ninth and Broadway that had "STOP" written on them. The signals must be stuck. Won't "GO" ever appear? I thought impatiently. Looking down Broadway, I saw the United Artists Theater. We had gone to the UA only once, but I wished we could go again, I had said, because "...it's so beautiful." Mother had explained that it was the last of twelve theaters built on Broadway that were intended to rival the theater district of New York's Great White Way.

Mother could keep me informed of other entertainment and crime news because of her theater background and current job with the District Attorneys office. I was the only child in third grade that knew John Wayne was "discovered" in his late teens while working as a set designer's "gopher" at Hollywood's Mack Sennett movie studio. That's where he was nicknamed "The Duke." On the other hand, "Rattlesnake James" got his nickname after being convicted, and ultimately executed, for killing his wife by putting her arm into a cage of rattlesnakes.

She would answer my questions whether or not she knew the correct answers. When I noticed that the sidewalk in front of the UA always seemed empty compared to the crowds near the Orpheum and the Eastern Columbia, I asked her why? She looked unsure, shrugged and said, " Well, I guess it's on the wrong side of Ninth. Maybe people just don't like to cross the street."

When it was finally safe for us to cross to the eastside of Broadway she said, "Let's go," then pulled me across the street. Once on the sidewalk, she freed my hand, which hurt from the pressure of her grip. I ran in front of her, reached the box office first, and waited for her to join me at the end of the short line for tickets.

"One adult and one child, please," Mother told the uniformed cashier confined inside a glass cage.

Purchasing tickets had become a nightmare for me. During the previous three summer vacation months I had gown three inches and now measured five feet, six inches, looked older, and was the tallest student in school, except for a six-foot fifth grader whom everyone avoided, convinced he was a real giant. I was unsuccessful when I tried to shrivel down in height to avoid the cashier challenging my age.

"You have to pay full price for her," she told my mother.

Outraged, Mother insisted that I was eight and refused to pay the higher price for children twelve and over. Mother won. As we walked toward the polished brass doors leading inside, she warned me, "You are going to be an Amazon."

"What's that?" I had just read the child's version of Victor Hugo's The Hunchback of Nortre Dame, and imagined turning into a deformed bell ringer.

Still angry, she said, "Look it up in the encyclopedia under Africa."

I was relieved. At least it wasn't French.

Once inside, she handed our tickets to an usher. He looked

at each ticket, at me, paused, then discreetly accepted the tickets -
Thank you God - tore them in half, and returned the stubs to my
mother who rewarded him with her 1920's flapper coquette smile.
I could hardly wait to be twelve. Then Mother would have to pay
full price for me. *Life will be so much easier.*

We walked into wonderland. The opulence of the brass
doors we passed through only hinted at the magnificence that
greeted us in the lobby. We stopped to admire the heavy drapery
and lush fabrics on walls not already covered by fine wood. Huge
columns of matching dark wood seemed to support these walls.
The chandeliers were so big I wondered how anyone could put
them up on the ceiling.

I was embarrassed, though, by several bare-breasted figures.
"Why don't they put clothes on those statues?"

" Because they're called 'art', Mother said.

"Dawn, let's go downstairs to the ladies room before the
show starts." Descending the wide, winding stairway, my mother
seemed transformed into a Ziegfeld showgirl, creating a sym-
phony of sensuality in her walk. But then, Mother was always on
stage, forever playing to an unseen audience.

I followed, imagining as I walked down each step what it
would be like to slide down the wooden banister that curved in
a gentle descent before it ended at what looked like an oversized
formal living room. This area was carpeted, and furnished with
comfortable furniture facing a mock fireplace. At the far end, a
ladies restroom had walls and floors of black marble laced with
tiny veins of white. A maid dressed in black with a white lace
cap and apron sat just inside. She was paid in tips from those
who could afford it. Since my mother earned only eighty-five
dollars a month, she said as we left that she did not feel obligated
to contribute.

If descending the Orpheum's stairway turned mother into
a showgirl, ascending I became an Olympic athlete, skipping two
stairs at a time, with an occasional attempt at three.

"You're going to fall, Dawn. Slow down," Mother cautioned, finally catching up with me at the top landing. From here we went to the door of the Orpheum's auditorium and glanced inside. "Certainly looks more like an opera house than a movie theater to me," she said. "It's so...baroque."

"Guess so." I had never been to an opera and didn't know what "baroque" meant. Since I didn't want to look it up, I didn't ask.

At the door, an usher with a flashlight offered to escort us to our seats. Mother thanked him, but said we could find our own way. Despite the crowd, we found two vacant seats together, one on the aisle. As usual, Ted Lewis would play to a full house.

As soon as we were comfortable, Mother handed me her purse.

"Hold this," she said as she got up, "don't talk to anyone, and don't get out of your seat while I'm gone. I'll be right back."

Before I could answer, she walked to the back of the theater. I watched her speak to the usher and give him something. It looked like a small piece of paper, but I couldn't be sure. He smiled and nodded. She turned and started back down the aisle.

It had been the first time I could remember her leaving me alone in public. Since the 1932 Lindbergh baby kidnapping, mother was terrified for my safety and saw each male stranger as a Bruno Hauptmann, the baby's convicted kidnapper. My current argument for independence was that I was eight - almost nine - grown to my new gargantuan height, and certainly not baby-cute any more. Besides, I would say, aren't we sort of poor? Who would want me? Mother's mind was set. So far, the Hall of Justice was the only place I was allowed to be by myself because "... Sheriff's deputies are all over the building."

She sat down, kissed my cheek, and squeezed my hand as she sunk back into her seat. She sighed, obviously relieved to see me where she left me. I knew better than to ask what she gave the usher.

The movie was about to begin. The next several hours would be the best part of my life.

Slowly, the lights dimmed then went out as the gold curtain parted and revealed a movie screen that would show us one movie, the news, and a short subject before Ted Lewis appeared on stage. I was usually restless, but sat like stone throughout the entire show, reluctant for it to end.

Between the movie and news I asked Mother to take me to the restroom.

"Can't you wait?" she said.

"No."

"Then let's hurry so we don't miss the news."

We got back to our seats just as the Pathe News rooster crowed "Cock-a-doodle-doo," Hollywood's barnyard introduction to news of war, President Roosevelt and beauty pageants. I was glad that my Republican grandmother was home and she would not be hearing Democrat Roosevelt applauding the courage of depression victims and talking about unrest in other countries. After several years she was still despondent that Republican President Herbert Hoover had lost the election to FDR. She blamed the elected Democratic president "...for this whole money mess," and added that "now he'll probably have our boys killed in some godforsaken place we never heard of."

I only tolerated the news. My love was the short subjects and I was transfixed through those fifteen or twenty minutes they were on the screen. Today they featured Robert Benchley, my favorite, a short, round man whose serious delivery contrasted with his sharp wit.

As the audience laughed at and applauded Benchley's last joke, the curtain was drawn across the screen, and the theater became dark and still. Quiet strains of music came from behind the gold curtain that parted as the music grew louder and a second gauze screen came into view. Now barely visible was what to me looked like fifty musicians playing the theme song of the bandleader we had come to see. The strains of <u>When My Baby Smiles At Me</u> filled the theater, moving us to new heights of cheers and applause.

From off stage his familiar voice began singing, "*When my baby smiles at me,*" and the audience grew silent. Half way through the next line - "*I go a wandering to paradise*" - Ted Lewis appeared on stage, smiled and strutted, waved his cane, and with a flick of his finger, adjusted his battered black top hat, while his free hand "danced" to the music and lyrics. For a few seconds the audience went wild, then quiet again as this "Medicine Man For Your Blues" finished talk-singing his song. I felt he was singing it just to me. I looked around at an audience obviously in love with this man who loved them back.

And my mother? For the first time at a Ted Lewis show, I saw her dabbing her eyes with a white handkerchief, then held it to her mouth as tears occasionally ran down her cheeks.

I put my hand on her arm. "Mommy, what's wrong?"

"Nothing...nothing, Dawn." She blew her nose and stuffed the handkerchief back into her purse. She smiled at me and laughed at the next funny thing Ted Lewis said. This was the first time I had ever seen her carry a handkerchief. It was as if she knew beforehand that she was going to cry.

With the upbeat <u>Alexander's Ragtime Band</u>, we both forgot her tears. By the time Ted Lewis was singing, <u>Wear a Hat With a Silver Lining</u>, we were completely mesmerized by the miracle happening on stage. Then the beautiful <u>Three O'Clock in the Morning</u> was performed behind the gauze screen as the orchestra played while ballroom dancers waltzed under a muted midnight-blue haze.

The audience could not get enough of Ted Lewis and his music. He could sing or talk his songs. Or combine the two. He could twirl his cane or play his clarinet, or both. Talk to his audience. Lead his band. Say his famous "Yes sir." Let his hat drop from his head onto his arm and roll into his hand, or introduce his acts. It did not matter. Whatever Ted Lewis did, he created a rapport with his adoring audience. When he came to the edge of the stage and asked his promised question, "Is everybody happy?" "Yes" came from everyone.

Then, as Me and My Shadow began, Ted Lewis and a man stepped from the wings in front of the screen's white background. They were dressed alike in black tuxedos with white carnations in the jacket lapels, white shirts with black bow ties, and high hats. The "shadow" was slightly shorter and walked a few steps in back of him. Both turned their profiles to the audience, and each one carried an identical cane.

Ted Lewis had begun singing the words just before he and the shadow were on stage. As he finished the first line and was ready to sing, "*strolling down the avenue,*" both men and their shadows were in full view on the screen. As Ted Lewis sang his way across the stage, his human shadow followed him exactly in sync with each of his movements, casting shadows that did the same. They seemed to climb invisible stairs, then knock at an imaginary door at the top. Their feet took steps forward and then quickly back. The cane followed that movement in time with their feet. Lewis' casual slight shimmy of shoulders was duplicated by his shadow as if these two were one. When they reached the far end of the stage, Ted Lewis ended his song with, "*...all alone and feeling blue,*" while he and his shadow walked into the wings. The audience had fallen in love all over again and gave him a standing ovation.

As they left the stage, I thought of something new to add to my own Me and My Shadow production at home. Between "*not a soul to tell our troubles to*" and " *When It's twelve o'clock we climb the stairs,*" I would give a flick of my finger on its brim to adjust my top hat. *It will look great.* I could hardly wait to get home and try it out.

Since there were often children at a Ted Lewis performance, the last part of the show was for us. Mother told me once that he loved kids but had never had any of his own, so this part was very special. As the house lights came on, Lewis came back on stage and walked close to the edge. The man who had played his shadow was now pushing an old-fashioned popcorn cart filled with peanuts. He would usually throw them into the audience where children scrambled for them. Instead, Ted Lewis walked to the middle of the stage and began talking, something I never heard him do before.

"Ladies and gentlemen," he began, "at this time I would like to invite all the children in the audience to come up on stage so I can meet each one of you personally."

I was so excited I jumped up from my seat and was going to run up on stage without asking my mother's permission. I was sure she would want me to go.

"Sit down," Mother said, without looking at me.

I just stared at her for a few seconds and was too shocked to ask, "Why?" Obediently, I climbed back over her knees and sat in my seat, too stunned to talk. Silently, I watched the other children climb the steps onto the stage, get their share of peanuts, and meet Ted Lewis, the most wonderful man in the world. *Mommy, why can't I go?*

Mother and I waited for the crowd to thin out before we got out of our seats to leave. I kept thinking only one other thing as I remembered my Mothers refusal to let me meet Ted Lewis. *There must be something wrong with me.*

We were both silent as the yellow streetcar rolled back to Highland Park, over Broadway, then Figueroa, and finally return to Avenue 52 where we got off and walked to our half of our rented duplex. That night I went to bed thinking, I guess I'll never be good enough to meet Ted Lewis.

Suddenly, I remembered something from a long time ago when I was very small. I knew then that I already had met Ted Lewis, and fell happily to sleep.

Chapter Three

"When The Moon Comes Over The Mountain"

I was three years old and this was a special occasion at the orphanage where I was living after my father died. Two famous people, we heard, were coming to visit us.

The other children were about my age, and we all sat in small chairs placed around a low round table. I am not sure we knew what "famous people" meant, but I was excited after we heard their names. I had never seen either one of them before, but I had heard their names mentioned several times by my grandmother and by my mother and my father. That was before he died.

As Ted Lewis and Kate Smith walked in the room together, I noticed that their clothes were the same color: pearl gray with accents of white. Ted Lewis wore a tuxedo with tails, a white shirt, and a very old black top hat. *He needs to buy a new hat.* Kate Smith and her theme song, When the Moon Comes Over the Mountain, were popular at home, especially for my grandmother. Kate Smith was a heavy woman in a long dress with long sleeves and a white Peter Pan collar. She wore no hat and her short, light brown hair was in tight finger waves. Ted Lewis came over to our table, while Kate Smith stood in a nearby corner. Both were smiling, happy people. They made me feel good. I did not recall anything more about Kate Smith.

It was Ted Lewis who I remember best, and the way he gave his entire attention to us children. I do not recall specific words or music, but I was aware of him singing and dancing around our table. Occasionally, he would bend down to hug and speak to each child. When he spoke to me, I truly felt such joy, and a sense that, for some unknown reason, he loved us all.

Chapter Four

"Maybe, Who Knows"

Mother's wake-up kiss Monday morning after our Sunday trip to see Ted Lewis was right on time: 7:30 a.m. It gave her enough time for me to dress for school and have breakfast with her before she left for work. Buying groceries and fixing meals was my grandmother's job. Mother and I sat at the break-fast nook in the kitchen while Grandma served us eggs and toast. The toast was a light brown color, but I knew it had been black, burned because I heard her scraping it while I was still in bed. Every morning that scratching of burned toast was my alarm to get up.

Mother asked, "Would you like coffee, Dawn?"

"Yes, please," I said.

"Mama, Dawn needs a cup." Mother got up from the table. She had finished her own coffee and left her mother to pour mine.

My grandmother scowled, grabbed a cup and saucer from the cupboard, and plunked them in front of me. In silent outrage, she handed the coffeepot to my mother, then said, "Here, you pour it. She has no business having coffee this young." She turned to me and glared. "Don't you know it will stunt your growth, young lady?"

That same routine had continued ever since my eighth

birthday when Mother gave me permission to have coffee, insisting I use lots of cream and sugar, as if they magically turned the brew into a confection and absolved her of guilt. My grandmother's threat of retarded growth never deterred me from drinking coffee, nor did her other two warnings that followed.

"The coffee is black, you know, and children who drink it before they are adults turn black. Is that what you want?" Her prediction did not refer to race, but to actual color. If coffee had been red, she would have said that my skin would turn red, or yellow, or blue, or any other color she might choose as a warning. "And you'll get wrinkles on your forehead." Since my complexion was already dark olive, and I was too young to worry about wrinkles, I ignored her arguments until the next day when she would repeat them. At mid point of Grandma's harangue, Mother would also ignore her warnings, bend down to kiss me goodbye, then tell us both that she would see us at dinner.

Usually, my grandmother was kind and gentle, and was considered an "angel-on-earth" to our friends and family, including me. Except after breakfast. Her anger from the conflict over coffee always spilled over into our next early morning event that involved my hair.

Mother insisted that my dark brown hair be worn in long, corkscrew curls, which had to be combed, then brushed around my grandmother's finger each morning before I went to school. Long curls was a style common during the 1930's to young girls whose mothers envisioned their daughters as Shirley Temple look-a-likes, taught them to sing, On the Good Ship Lollipop, and prepared them for movie stardom.

Despite my natural curly hair, Mother insisted I have permanent waves, a beauty process I considered an unnecessary agony. Despite my protests, she dragged me every few months to a full day's torture at the beauty shop, where my head was mana-cled to a tall machine with long, squid-like tentacles of electrical cord that produced unbearable heat. The result was kinky hair, snarled and difficult to comb. Faced daily with this tangled mop, my grandmother seemed possessed by Satan as she attacked each lock with vengeance.

"Ouch," I yelled. "You're hurting me."

"Hush," she said, "it's your imagination."

"Please, stop pulling." As the yanks got more severe with each complaint, she was undaunted. By the time she finished, my tears were followed by screams that threw her into more intense rage. "Someday, young lady," she said, "you'll end up in a reformatory."

This morning we were both silent and not speaking when my friend, Sally, rang the doorbell and asked, "What's wrong, Dawn?" She could hear me screaming, she said, and asked if I was ready to walk to school?

"Nothing's wrong," I said. "I'm ready."

As we left, Grandma handed me my lunch, grumbled goodbye, and kissed me as if she were sending me off to jail.

By the time I returned home in the afternoon, both of us had forgotten our anger and kissed as I came into the living room. She seemed genuinely glad I was not in juvenile hall. At last my angel grandmother was back.

"Cookies are in the kitchen, Dawn. Bring them in here. I want to hear all about the Ted Lewis show yesterday."

We sat close together on the couch. As we ate cookies, she asked more questions as I told her every detail, including that Mother did not allow me to meet Ted Lewis.

"Please don't tell Mommy I told you that part. Promise?"

"Of course I promise." She hugged me and told me to have another cookie. Then she became very serious. "Dawn, were you disappointed not to meet him?"

"Oh, yes." I finished my cookie, then asked for another. "At first."

Grandma gave me a fourth cookie despite her usual limit of three. We both were silent as I ate.

"But, when I got in bed last night, I thought about something that made me feel really good." I told her all about Ted Lewis and Kate Smith visiting the orphanage when I was little. When I finished my story, I added, "I wish I could have talked to him yesterday. I wonder if he still remembers me? Grandma, can I go play with Sally now?"

She did not answer.

"We have to finish our <u>Easy Money</u> game at her house," I said. "She's waiting for me. Can I go now?"

"Soon, dear," she said. When Grandma called me "dear," I knew I could expect something unusual. *I probably won't get to finish our game today. I might as well get back on the couch. This is going to take a long time.*

When I sat down again, Grandma waited a few seconds, turned to me and told me to look at her. Her voice was very calm and sweet. "Dawn, why didn't you ever tell us about Ted Lewis and Kate Smith before?"

"I don't know," I said, confused by the question. "I hardly ever think about it. It was such a long time ago." I picked up a few cookie crumbs off the plate that was now empty. "Is it important?"

"Well, it's just that we didn't even know you remembered when you were so young. Or even being at the orphanage.

"Sure I do," I said. "I really liked it there. There were so many children to play with."

"What else do you remember?"

"Oh, lots. Especially the time I threw up in my soup at dinner and they took me to the hospital. Wasn't that when I had diphtheria?" I started laughing as I told her how mad the nurse was because I wouldn't eat my oatmeal. "I can remember things when I was even more little."

"'Younger', Dawn, not 'more little.'" Grandma was firm about using correct words. "You remember being... sick?" She was a devout Christian Scientist and usually avoided the names of diseases. Even the word "sick" stuck in her throat. "Are you sure you weren't just dreaming about Ted Lewis and Kate Smith?"

I was getting a little upset with her. She sounded as though she didn't believe me.

"Grandma, I know the difference between a dream and when something really happens. A dream is like the time when I was three. Mommy was in night school, and I fell out of my crib. I thought she was spraying her throat with that weird bottle she uses while she was sitting in bed. I climbed over my crib railing to get into bed with her and fell on the floor. I remember that I cried and those other people in the house tried to help me. Mommy wasn't even home yet. That's a dream. I hadn't ever seen Ted Lewis or Kate Smith before they came to the orphanage. I'd only heard about them from you and Mommy. They were real, Grandma."

"Oh, Dawn, of course you know what a dream is. But, you've never talked about any of this before." When she put her arms around me, I thought she was going to cry. But, Grandma was tough and laughed instead. "Wait 'til your mother hears about this."

"Grandma, you promised not to tell. It might really upset her."

"You're right. This is our secret. It would upset her."

"Now, grandchild mine, are there any other secrets in that grown up mind of yours that I should know?"

"Well, maybe. I'll think about it," I gave her a big hug. "Can I go to Sally's first? I was just about to win Easy Money."

"Go, go," she said, shooing me out of the house. "Promise you won't eat any of her baloney sandwiches and spoil your dinner. No popcorn soaked in buttermilk, either." Sally's favorite foods were always a mystery to Grandma.

I ran out the door and down our steps. "I promise," I called back. I was already planning my memory list to tell Grandma. I could hardly wait to tell her about the time when I was in my stroller at Venice Beach. *Grandma will love that one.*

Chapter Five

"Oh Baby"

*A*fter I tell Grandma my Venice Beach stroller story, she'll know
that I really did remember Ted Lewis being at the orphanage.

Venice Beach was overcast when my mother parked her
Packard in front of a large building with several tall archways
that bordered and covered the sidewalk along the side of the
building. Charlotta, my nanny's eighteen-year-old daughter,
had come with us. As if both were teenagers, they chattered and
giggled as they unloaded my light green stroller and placed me on
its long wooden seat.

"You really remember that old building with the arches, and
your baby stroller?" Grandma stopped eating her cookie. "Dawn,
how could you? You wouldn't even get into that stroller after you
were two and a half. We never could figure out why."

It was a few days after I promised Grandma to tell her
about my earliest memories. It was after school and we were again
sitting in the backyard swing, and had become our afternoon
ritual.

"Oh, I remember even before that," I said as I pushed the
swing harder with both feet. "I think we still lived in Hollywood,
and someone would push me in it by a white picket fence."

"That's right. That fence was across the street from the
Kingsley apartments in Hollywood. Your mother and father lived

there when you were born." Grandma put down her cookie and looked at me. " Do you remember him? Your daddy?"

"A little. I think I remember him after we moved from Hollywood because we were living in a house with a yard." I thought a few moments before I told her, "I never felt he liked me very much."

She hesitated a few seconds. "Of course Fred liked you," she said. Your father loved you, dear."

I knew I was right. She called me "dear."

Grandma set the empty cookie dish on the grass, settled back into the swing, and gave it a push with her own feet to keep it swinging. "Now, for the rest of your Venice story."

"Well, Charlotta and Mommy pushed me out to that wide sidewalk that goes along the edge of the sand. Then they got on the back end of the Venice Tram so that they were looking backwards instead of forward. Grandma, you know how that tram that goes along the beach that's all open, sort of like that trolley car we rode in San Francisco?"

Grandma laughed. "Your mother always did like to sit back there and ride backwards. But, there's no room back there for a stroller. Where did they put it?"

"Nowhere," I said. "Mommy left the stroller, with me in it, on the sidewalk while she sat in the back of the tram with Charlotta. When the tram started to move, well, Mommy held onto its handle and pulled me along with the tram."

"She...what?" I never saw my grandmother so shocked. "She didn't hold you on her lap? That tram goes pretty fast along the beachfront when it gets going. What if she'd let loose of the handle? You could have been killed."

"I never thought of that. But, I sure remember how I was so scared. And the tram just kept going faster and faster. Everything was rushing by me...backwards. I cried and screamed. I thought it would never stop. I don't remember my stroller at all after that."

"That's probably why you wouldn't get in it again."

Grandma got out of the swing and started toward the house. "Time to fix dinner. Want to help me shell peas?"

"Sure."

"Don't forget to whistle. You can't eat up my raw peas and whistle at the same time."

As we went into the kitchen, I was glad that two good things happened. Now I was going to eat a lot of raw peas, and was sure Grandma believed me about remembering Ted Lewis.

Chapter Six

"Keep Sweeping The Cobwebs Off Of The Moon"

Grandma became ill and died when I was ten. I never knew my grandmother to be sick, not from a cold or headache, until a few months before she collapsed unconscious on our living room couch. Mother called Dr. Ryan who examined her as she sat up in bed.

"You're doing just fine," he told her. "But, Olive, you're going to have to stay in bed a few days until I take some tests. Okay?"

Grandma said, "Of course, Doctor." I knew Grandma would be out of bed as soon as he left.

"Mama, you've got to stop running around. Remember what Dr. Ryan told you?" My mother was worried about Grandma who refused to follow the doctor's orders to stay home and in bed. She had already had two more attacks like the first, had been diagnosed with a leaky heart, but refused to slow down her activities.

"Ruth, I'm fine. Besides, our July Fourth party at the Townsend Club is in a few days, and I'm playing piano for the entertainment. Did you forget that Dawn is doing 'Ted Lewis'? We just can't miss it."

Mother winced when Grandma said, "Ted Lewis," the first time I ever saw her not smile when his name was mentioned. But all she said was, "I remember. You know I can't drive you there. It's too strenuous for you to walk and then take the streetcar in your condition."

I knew Mother was right. I also knew there was nothing she could do to keep her mother at home. My grandmother believed, "Mornings are for the house; afternoons are for getting out of the house and seeing what the world's all about; late afternoons and evenings are for needlework, reading, seeing a movie or listening to the radio."

She had three loves that fitted in with this philosophy: visiting her friends; going to the library; and supporting the Townsend Club. In 1934, Dr. Francis E. Townsend introduced an old age pension plan to those gathered at Bixby Park that overlooks the Pacific Ocean in Long Beach, California. The elderly, he said, should be given "...two hundred dollars a month for the rest of their lives." Within a few years, the Townsend Plan led to a United States national Social Security program.

"That's ridiculous, Mama," my mother argued. "I only make eighty-five dollars a month and work six days a week. You expect to get more than twice as much as I do?"

Grandma was undaunted. "We've worked hard all of our lives and deserve an adequate income when we get old." Consequently, nothing could keep her from the local club meetings, and I often went with her. There were always lots of grandchildren running around. We had fun playing during the boring speeches, and looked forward to wonderful food served by these seniors after their meetings. Since this and her other activities all involved walking and riding public transportation, Mother considered them disastrous to her mother's failing health.

She would, however, enjoy one more Townsend Club meeting despite my mother's warning to stay home. Nothing would keep her from playing the piano for her friends, and also for me as I performed a solo Ted Lewis act (despite my pleadings and promises, Sally refused to join me.) This was my grandmother's final meeting, and the last time I would sing <u>Me and My Shadow</u> with her playing the piano as I walked across a makeshift stage, and asked at the end, "Is everybody happy"? A few weeks later she was buried at Forest Lawn Memorial Park in Glendale, California.

Chapter Seven

"Down The Old Church Aisle"

Deputy Sheriff Roy Rankin was retiring from the Los Angeles County Sheriff's Office after twenty-eight years of service. While he would leave behind no accolades as "Most Liked Deputy on the Force" (one fellow officer dubbed him "Bigot of the Year"), his achievements as a county law enforcement officer from 1911 to 1939 were worthy of merit.

Early in his career he had helped establish a spirit of cooperation between law enforcement and the press. Rankin had been working arson detail and had become acquainted with Daniel Green, one of the foremost Los Angeles journalists at the time. In tracking arson statistics, the sheriff's office had discovered an important fact regarding purposely set fires. Whenever they were reported in the newspapers as arson, these incidents increased. Conversely, when their actual cause was not given, and they were reported simply as "fires," the number of Los Angeles County arsons decreased. The sheriff's office determined that reporting fires as arson triggered something in potential arsonist to set more fires. To deter this fire activity, Deputy Rankin was directed to convince local reporters not to print any fires as caused by arson when they wrote their news stories. Reporters agreed to comply. Subsequent arson stories contained no mention of the cause. Incidents of arson substantially decreased.

Deputy Sheriff Rankin also was hopelessly in love with guns and was top marksman in the department for several years, and his home was an arsenal. In each room, including the bathrooms, he kept at least one gun.

What almost ruined his career, however, was a secret assignment that took him over the border into Tijuana, Mexico. In pursuit of two fugitives who sought escape from the United States in Mexico, Rankin was sent below the border to capture them. When he found them, a gunfight ensued, they shot him, escaped, and left him for dead.

Tijuana police found the deputy lying unconscious and took him to jail. They incarcerated him for three days in a cell without medical help, supposing him to be the felon.

"When I came to in that goddamned-cold-dirty-jail with just a board to lie on, I figured I was just about dead. Blood all over the place. A hole as big as a fist in my chest. I couldn't breath. I knew I was going to die, but I just kept saying to my self, over and over, 'I am not going to die in this goddamned-dirty-rotten-hellhole'. For three days ...and I could hardly talk... I pleaded with them to get a doctor and call the sheriff's office in L.A. so they'd know who I was. I wasn't in uniform so I was just a plain god-damned criminal to them. Finally they called the sheriff's department to come and get me.

"I lost a lung in that one and was sent to Canada for a year to recuperate. Never will breath right again, goddamn-it."

When Los Angeles newspapers ran the story, they reported that Deputy Sheriff Roy Rankin was killed in a gun shoot-out in Tijuana. The United States government hoped to avoid an international conflict with Mexico if the world thought he was dead.

Still alive and planning retirement, Deputy Rankin had two goals. The first was to establish a water company where he lived in Baldwin Park, an unincorporated town just east of Los Angeles city limits. His second goal was to marry Ruth Whipple.

Chapter Eight

"They'll Be Some Changes Made"

A few months before Grandma died, Mother changed our lives. "Mama, Dawn...Dawn, don't turn on the radio yet... sit down. I have something to tell you." Mother looked strangely serious as she directed Grandma and me to the couch. I was already at the radio, but obeyed her and sat down next to my grandmother. *Did I do something wrong?*

Grandma and I had recently worked out our morning hair-pulling problem when I announced that I was going to wash and comb my own hair. No more curls. No more morning pain. I felt like I had reached adulthood when they both agreed I was old enough to take care of my own hair. *Mommy must be mad at me for something else.*

Several long seconds passed before my mother spoke.

"I'm going to marry Roy Rankin."

Both Grandma and I were speechless. The silence that continued seemed like hours before my mother spoke again.

"You can turn on the radio now, Dawn."

I went to the radio, turned it on and turned the dial to the Jack Benny show. Jack Benny said, "Jello, again," his way of advertising the program's sponsor, Jello. I was glad we missed only the introduction and would hear most of the show. Grandma and I were going to need some cheering up after my mother's bomb that just blew up our lives.

Grandma finally recovered. "Ruth, he's married. How can you?"

"He's getting divorced, Mama. In a month he'll retire and then go to Nevada to start divorce proceedings and his six-week residency in Reno. He's already told his wife and asked her to move."

Grandma did not answer. She finally rose from the couch and said, "Ruth, I think I'll go to bed early. Goodnight, dear. Goodnight, Dawn." Grandma kissed and hugged me until I thought I'd break She never again discussed her daughter marrying this man whom I knew she disliked.

"Dawn, it's a school day tomorrow. You need to go to bed, too. Right after 'Jack Benny'," Mother said.

I obeyed without my usual Sunday night argument to stay up later, and my mother tucked me into bed. Neither of us mentioned her getting married. She kissed me and closed my door as she left my room.

As soon as I was sure my mother would not return to check up on me, I got out of bed, went into my tiny clothes closet, and shut the door so I knew my mother could not hear me. For at least an hour I sobbed in my black sanctuary. *She can't marry him...she just can't.* I always had wanted a father more than anyone knew. Every once in a while, when walking home from school I would pretend that may father was still alive and I would meet him around the next corner. I also wanted my mother to have a husband and not have to work anymore. But Roy Rankin was not the kind of man I thought she would marry. I did not dislike him as my grandmother did. I just knew that the fun and joy in our life would be gone and everything would be changed. My mother must never know that I felt by marrying Roy Rankin she was turning out the bright light in our lives.

Mother, about 19, and Colonel Diamond perform "Youth and Old Age," Vaudeville, in 1920

My mother, Ruth Olive Dean, circa 1920.

***

After Mother's first date with Deputy Rankin, the short, stocky, gray-haired officer became a familiar figure in our home, always wearing his olive-drab uniform, badge, and, to Grandma's horror, his gun. Standing next to my mother who was still very attractive (*Why can't I be pretty and look like my mother. And why don't I looked like someone...anyone... in our family?*), his stern and not-so-good-looking face above a protruding belly made them a strange looking couple. He was almost twenty years older than she and appeared to be her father rather than her date. At thirty-nine Mother still looked like a young woman.

Mr. Rankin, as I called him, was friendly to me and at ease, not trying to impress me as a possible future father candidate.

"Dawn, do you like animals?" he asked one evening while waiting for mother to finish dressing for their date.

"Oh, yes," I said. Especially dogs and horses. I'm going to have a horse some day, and a Collie." Mother and Grandma had been hearing my desire for a Collie and horse for so long my requests fell on deaf ears. Mr. Rankin seemed genuinely interested and made me think that maybe he wasn't so bad after all.

After they left, Grandma asked, "Dawn, do you like that man?"

"I don't know. I guess he's okay. Guess what, Grandma, he used to be a racehorse jockey."

Grandma looked at me again. "He said damn, didn't he?"

"Yes, Grandma, he did."

She never said anything about Roy Rankin to me again. She didn't have to. I knew how she felt about people who said "damn."

When Mr. Rankin again came to take my mother out, I answered the door.

"Here, Dawn, this is for you," and handed me one end of a dog leash attached to a collar on the most beautiful Collie I ever saw. And this is for your mother. His other hand held what I thought was a tall, green bottle of ginger ale.

Soon my mother walked in.

"Here, Ruth, this is a bottle of <u>Sake</u> from my Japanese neighbors, the Yokoe's. They have the truck garden land across the street from me. Put it in the refrigerator and we'll have a drink before we leave."

Just then Grandma came in and said, "Oh, hello, Roy, won't you sit down?"

He greeted her, asked her if she was feeling better, and reminded Mother about the <u>Sake</u>.

"Pour us a couple of glasses before we leave. Oh, Mrs. Dean. Would you like a glass of <u>Sake</u> with us?"

"What's that?" Grandma said.

"Japanese whiskey."

Grandma, the Teetotaler, could barely get out the words, "No, thank you." Then Mother brought in two juice glasses half filled with Sake. She gave one to Mr. Rankin, they clicked their glasses, and said "cheers" before they drank. My grandmother was obviously in utter disbelief, but sat without comment through the ritual. She pretended to read her book that she held more like a life preserver than literature. Then Mr. Rankin pulled out a package of Camel cigarettes, offered one to my mother who took one and lit it, and then to my grandmother. If the cigarette had been straw, this would have been the one that "...broke the camel's back." Liquor, tobacco, and profanity, the things she hated most, were being flaunted right in front of her and her granddaughter by her own daughter. Still in control, however, she rose from the couch, said goodnight to Mr. Rankin, and went to bed.

Swearing, <u>Sake</u>, and cigarette stubs became permanent fixtures in our home. A <u>Sake</u> bottle was always in full view when Grandma opened the refrigerator, ashtrays on our coffee table always needed to be emptied, and Deputy Rankin's profanity increased with each complaint from Grandma. Even my mother's caution to curb his swearing was useless. He seemed delighted to irritate his future mother-in-law.

The Collie, which I named Sheila, and I fell in love immediately, but we were separated within a month.

"Your mother thinks I should take Sheila out to my place in Baldwin Park. You can see her when you visit and she'll be there when you come to live with me."

I was heartbroken but knew better than to argue.

A couple of weeks later when Mother and I went out to Mr. Rankin's home, as soon as we got out of the car I looked for Sheila who did not come when I called her.

"She's been gone for a couple of days," he said, "but I'm sure she'll be back soon, Dawn."

For the next few hours I looked and called everywhere I could think of for my Collie. There was no answer and I went into the house, heart broken that I did not find her. I never saw Sheila again.

*****

Mother became Mrs. Roy Rankin in Reno, Nevada, a few weeks after Grandma died. A woman was hired to stay with me until they returned from their honeymoon. Just before they got in the car to leave, Mother took me into my bedroom and shut the door.

"Dawn, there's something you have to promise me. Don't ever mention Ted Lewis again. I've already torn up his picture and thrown it away."

"But, why, Mommy, can't I talk about him? Why did you tear it up? You loved that picture. And...you mean I can't do my Ted Lewis song anymore...ever?"

"No, never. All you need to know is, that Roy doesn't like who he is."

"What's wrong with Ted Lewis?"

"Shep", Roy Rankin and my mother, Ruth Whipple Ramkin, at home in Baldwin Park, California.

"Never mind. That's all you need to know. Do you promise?"

"Well, yes, but I don't see why..."

"You don't need to, okay? Now, do you promise?"

"All right, I promise."

"Good. Now come here and give me a big goodbye kiss and wish me luck."

Roy Rankin and Ruth Whipple drove out of the driveway to get married and begin their new life together.

Three weeks later they turned into the same driveway as Mr. and Mrs. Roy Rankin. Somewhere in Auburn, California while driving on steep curves, their car went over a cliff and rolled down several hundred feet down the mountainside. My beautiful mother arrived home injured and would carry a long scar on her forehead for the rest of her life.

Chapter Nine

"Is Everybody Happy, Now?"

My Prince appeared when I was thirteen and a freshman at Covina Union High School in Covina, California, orange grove country seven miles east of Baldwin Park.

"I've got a surprise for you this afternoon, Dawn." My stepfather was stoking a fire now blazing in a black potbellied stove in our dinning room, a large elegant space befitting its French provincial dinning set, but incongruous with this primitive heater. We had two new gas floor furnaces, but ex-Deputy Sheriff Roy Rankin took pleasure in chopping wood for the stove, and the winter morning ritual of building and tending a fire.

"Reminds me of back home in Rosendale, Missouri," he said. This was the only good thing I ever heard him say about his hometown. "See you after school?"

"Okay," I said as I left for school, kissing both him and my mother who was still sitting at the table and finishing her breakfast. "Goodbye Mom, Dad. See you then," and walked out the door and to my bus stop.

Recently, I had reluctantly agreed to call my stepfather, "Dad," and was still uncomfortable with this too familiar sign of affection. But, it made my mother happy, and he also seemed pleased.

I learned to expect very little from my mother's new

husband and gave little thought to his "promise" of a surprise. By the time I returned home I had completely forgotten about it, changed my clothes, and started to read a new short story in Redbook magazine. Mother was ironing his work clothes, the only type of clothes he ever bought. He refused to purchase slacks and shirts, and wore only bib-overalls, work shirts, and khaki-colored farm-type pants held up by wide suspenders. Topped by an old, wide-brimmed straw hat, he looked like a refugee from the Dust Bowl.

"I spent twenty-eight years dressed in a goddamned uniform and no one's going to get me back in another straight jacket." Roy Rankin kept his promise.

"Is she home?" I heard him ask my mother as he came into the house.

"Yes, Roy. She's in the living room reading. Are you going to show her now?"

"Damn right. This is going to be one hell of a surprise. Come on out with us."

"Where are we going?" I asked Mother as she and I walked towards our oversize three-car garage. *Guess we're going to drive someplace. Wish I didn't have to go.*

Dad led us past the garages and beyond a small house he had built to store grain to feed Chester White pigs which he planned to buy and raise. He stopped at the long, wood gate attached to an electric fence around our soon-to-be pastureland for the pigs that included a small grove of eucalyptus trees along the far end of the property. Dad had planted them for firewood because their wood was hard, burned well, and grew back within a few years after the trees were cut down. "Save a hell of a lot of money not having to plant new trees."

"Okay, Dawn, open the gate and go inside."

"But, I'll step on the new grass." He had planted the acreage in pasture grass for the expected pigs, and a new, green grass gave a lush to the ten acres it covered.

"It's okay," he said.

I opened the gate, careful not to touch the electric fence. I expected Mom and Dad to follow, but they stayed behind.

"Aren't you coming, too?" I asked, surprised to see them on the other side of the gate. "What do I do now?"

"What do you see?" Dad asked.

"Nothing," I said, "except grass, and the trees back there."

"Keep looking."

A shrill whistle pierced the air. I jumped, looked behind me, just as Dad blew another of his ear-splitting whistles between two fingers in his mouth. I glared at him for scaring me.

"There, in the trees. See that?"

I looked where he pointed. I had been getting nearsighted and the trees were a blur that suddenly began to move. Then I saw the blur leave the trees and come towards me, gaining speed until it stopped in front of me.

"A horse!" I screamed, stunned by the sight of the most beautiful animal I ever saw.

"Like him? He's called a Bay because of his red-brown color and black mane and tail. And he's a gelding. That's because he's a castrated male horse."

"Roy!" Mother yelled. My stepfather's sex description was too frank for her. "Can't you use a little discretion?"

"If she's old enough to have a horse, she sure as hell's old enough to know that her horse won't want to mate with a female horse. It makes them easier to manage, Dawn. They don't go around chasing women horses when the lady's in heat." He laughed at what he thought was a funny joke. Mother knew enough not to pursue this issue.

"Here's a couple of cube sugars. Now, watch me. See how I put them, one at a time, on the flat of my hand and hold it out to him?" The Bay put his nose on his hand and nuzzled the sugar into his mouth. Like a kid begging for more candy, he now brushed his nose against his arm. "Be sure you keep your hand flat—don't curl your fingers or they'll end up in his mouth, maybe in his stomach. Here, you try it."

I was scared. I fed him two sugars as Dad showed me, glowing inside as his velvet nose nuzzled my hand. Then I petted him, carefully at first, but gaining confidence as I saw how gentle he was.

"Don't walk directly in back of him in case he kicks. And watch those hoofs. It hurts like hell if he steps on your feet."

"Oh, by the way, his name's Prince. You can change it if you want, but he already knows his name."

" 'Prince' is great. And, thanks, Dad. I love him."

"Prince, it is. Tomorrow will see about getting you a saddle."

I could hardly wait to ride Prince, but it was a couple of days before Dad and I found the saddle and bridle he wanted.

"Dad, can I ride him after school today?"

"Prince and I'll be waiting for you, right after school."

That day I thought the bus would never get me home, and I ran to the house after it got to my stop.

"I'm home," I said to whomever might be around. "Just let me change clothes."

When my Levis were on, I found Dad in his chair in the living room.

"I'm ready," I said.

"Let's go, then."

We got Prince and Dad put the new saddle and bridle on him. "I'll teach you how to do this yourself tomorrow. Now, you lead him across the street to the Yokoe's land."

The Japanese truck garden across from our house had been vacated by the Yokoe family a year before when they were relocated to the Pomona fairgrounds which had been converted into a temporary Japanese internment camp after Pearl Harbor and the outbreak of World War Two. The Yokoes chose to relocate permanently in Colorado for the duration of the war, an option to relocate inland which had been given west coast Japanese if they were able to move to the interior of the United States. They had to forfeit their California land that was now occupied by people from Oklahoma. The property, once a bounty of greenery from the vegetables the Yokoes planted, was now a dry and barren wasteland.

"Always get on from the left side," Dad said, helping me put my left foot into the stirrup. "Now, put your left hand on this... that's a saddle horn...and pull yourself up and at the same time throw your right leg over the saddle."

It took several failures before I was successful and found myself sitting on my own horse for the first time. I was scared, but also felt that I had just conquered the world. Dad, however, was irritated that I did not do it the first time and was beginning to get impatient.

"Now, you're ready to ride. Hit him on the belly with the sides of your feet, say 'giddy up,' and go...oh, put your reins in your left hand. And remember, a good rider never hangs on to the saddle horn."

How am I going to remember all this?

I did everything Dad said, but Prince would not move. I tried again, again, and one more time before Dad got angry.

"Let him know who's boss. Dig your heels in harder, damnit."

"I'm trying, Dad. He just won't go." I glanced at Dad who was getting red in the face. I tried one more time, hitting him as hard as I could. Nothing.

"You goddamned little bitch. Get off and go in the house."

I got down, went into my room, and slammed the door. I fell face down onto my bed, my head buried in my pillow.

Mother came running into my room. "What's the matter, Dawn?"

"Dad called me a 'goddamn little bitch.'"

"He what?" Mother left the room as quickly as she came in.

As I lay there, a question from the past that I had not heard

for a long time flashed through my mind: "Is everybody happy?"
"*No.*"

Chapter Ten

"Poor Papa"

My wedding was set for August 26, 1950, two months after my June graduation from The University of California at Berkeley. I would marry Blake Williams, a rugged and handsome, twenty-two year old Mechanical Engineer student at Berkeley. He was from Bakersfield, oil and agricultural town in Central California's San Joaquin Valley that stretches some five-hundred miles between the Sierra Nevada mountains to the east and California's Coastal Range on the west, and was the setting for John Steinbeck's Depression era novel, <u>Grapes of Wrath</u>. It was a previous marriage engagement that brought back memories of when I lived with my mother and grandmother.

***

In my junior year at Berkeley, I became engaged to a young graduate student in Business Administration, who surprised me when he came to Baldwin Park during Christmas vacation to meet my mother and stepfather.

"I've got an idea for you and Verne when he gets here tomorrow," my mother said.

She and I were alone in the kitchen planning Christmas dinner.

"You and Dad seem to be pretty happy," I said. "Anything

to do with me being away at college?"

Mother smiled. "Well, Dawn, it is a lot easier than hearing you two argue whether or not FDR ruined the country. He still thinks he's '...raising a damned Democrat...' when he reads your letters."

"I guess I find it easier to live away, too. You know, I actually enjoy being home with him now that it's only for a short time. If he'd only stop blasting Democrats and Jews."

For an instant my mother frowned and looked sad, but quickly regained her smile and laughed. "Roy is Roy, and there's no changing him."

Right after breakfast Dad went to Pomona, a city about ten miles east of Baldwin Park, wearing his very oldest work clothes. He was going to buy a new Chrysler.

"I love to see who'll wait on me looking poor and penniless. Last time I did this it took almost thirty minutes before anyone offered to help me. I wish you could have seen the look on those guys' faces when I bought the most expensive car from him and paid cash. See you when I get back with my new Chrysler." He put on his old straw hat and left.

"Dawn, I read in the paper yesterday that Ted Lewis is playing at the Biltmore Bowl. Would you like me to call and get reservations for you and Verne to have dinner and see the show? You could take the bus."

Only once in the years since Mother and Roy Rankin had been married had I heard the name "Ted Lewis" in our home. Charlotta, Mother's long time friend, was visiting and I heard them talking about Ted Lewis, but they stopped when I entered the room.

"That would be great," I said. "But, what about Dad?"

"Neither you or Verne must ever mention where you're going. Just say 'to a movie and dinner in Los Angeles'. Do you understand?"

"Of course, Mom. And I'll make sure Verne does the same.

Okay?"

Mother looked serious. "Okay, and remember, this is the last we'll ever talk about it. You can pick up your tickets at the Biltmore when you get there." She smiled. "I already ordered them."

That night at the Biltmore Bowl, seeing Ted Lewis perform brought back happy memories of my life alone with my mother and grandmother. This time as he sang Me and My Shadow, I imagined a little three-year-old girl with dark curly hair and olive skin, wearing a black high hat and carrying a black cane, imitating every move that Ted Lewis made as she followed him across the stage. This time I'll be the shadow. That will be fun.

In January I gave Verne back his ring. I knew we did not love each other enough to marry.

***

A crisis arose one week before my wedding planned for "The Church of the Good Shepherd," a small Methodist chapel in Arcadia, a tiny town between Pasadena and Baldwin Park. Mother made my wedding dress. Mother and my six bridesmaids had their dresses. The flower girl's mother had finished the last touches on her daughter's white dress. We were all ready. Except Dad.

"Hell, no I'm not going to buy any goddamn suit just to wear once. Think I'm made of money? I've got plenty of clothes hanging in my closet."

"Don't worry, Dawn," my mother said, "Dad will change his mind and buy a suit. Let me talk to him,"

"Mom, don't forget new shoes, oh, and white shirt and tie. I don't know, Mom, you know how stubborn he is." I was worried. Only twice before had I won my way whenever we had differences. The first was when I decided on going to college at Berkeley, five hundred miles away. The second was milking the cow.

***

Despite Dad's crude stories, profanity, and unbridled temper, I knew he truly loved me. "He just doesn't know how to express it," I would tell myself when things became unbearable.

"Stay home to go to college," he pleaded. "Go to UCLA, USC, or Pomona, how about that one. You could even live here... it's close enough and I'll buy you a car. I'll send you anywhere you want down here. Just don't go away." Tears filling his eyes began rolling down his cheeks.

My answer was, "No." This was my one chance to leave home, live on my own, and be free from Dad. "I've already been accepted at Berkeley. Besides, it's too late to apply anywhere else." He could not argue against that.

My refusal to learn to milk a Jersey cow he bought, so that we and the pigs could have plenty of milk, had been a battle of wits and was the second issue that I won. *If I learn to milk this cow I'll have to do it two times a day, seven days a week, three hundred and sixty-five days a year for the rest of my life.*

Dad did not speak to me for two days after I ignored his demand that I learn to milk the cow, and it was never mentioned again. From then on, twice a day he milked the Jersey and stocked our refrigerator, now overcrowded with milk. The pigs were happy. My mother and I complained at washing the buckets. He sold the cow at the end of three months.

***

My wedding was Saturday night and by Thursday night Dad still had no suit. Neither Mother's urging nor my crying moved him. I was finally resigned to walk down the aisle on the arm of a father dressed for planting the North Forty instead of giving away his daughter at her church wedding. *At least he won't be wearing that awful straw hat.* For a brief moment I panicked. *What if he does?*

Sometime before noon on Friday, Mother rushed into my bedroom where I was packing for my honeymoon.

"Dawn, Dad's agreed to buy a suit. We're shopping for it after lunch."

I sat down on the bed in disbelief. "What happened? How did you get him to give in?"

"I told him I'd leave him and get a divorce if he didn't."

Dad's new suit, a soft medium brown, was delivered shortly after noontime on Saturday. By six o'clock he was dressed, including new shoes, white shirt, and tie. He looked wonderful.

The eight-thirty wedding was beautiful and I was proud to have Dad walk me down the aisle.

"Who gives this woman to be married to this man?" asked the minister.

"Her mother and I," Dad replied, then took his seat beside my mother and held her hand.

Our reception afterwards in the church recreation hall was filled with both families and friends. I noticed that Dad and his friends spent a good deal of their time together. I was happy that he was enjoying my wedding.

After Blake and I said goodbye to everyone, we drove to Riverside and spent our first night at the old Mission Inn, drove up California's coastline the next day to begin our week-long honeymoon, and finally returned to my parents home for a night. Blake had one more semester before getting his Engineer degree and we had to leave the next morning for Berkeley.

When we arrived in Baldwin Park, Mother came out to greet us.

"Where's Dad?" I asked my mother.

"He's in the living room. Oh, by the way, he's stopped smoking."

"Good. Now maybe he'll breathe easier." I walked into

the living room, said, "Hi," and kissed my stepfather who was sitting in his chair dressed in a handsome dark blue suit with coordinated shirt, tie, and shoes.

When Mother and I were alone I asked, "How come he's in a suit? Isn't that one new?"

"Well, at your reception every one of Dad's friends went on and on about him how great he looked in his new suit. You can't imagine how pleased he was. So, on Monday morning he told me that he was going to get another suit and would I go with him to help pick it out. We went to the same store where he got the brown one—by the way, he wore it that day—and he looked at several suits in other colors, but he couldn't make up his mind which one to buy. He asked me which one I liked and I said I liked them all. So, he took four different colored suits with shoes, shirts and ties to go with each one. Since then he puts on a different suit, shirt, tie, and shoes every morning and has thrown away his old clothes. Including his hat."

A month later I received a letter from my mother:

Dear Dawn,

You're not going to believe this! Since you and Blake got married, not only does dad put on a different suit every morning, including everything to go with it, we actually go to nice restaurants and a movie on Saturday night. Hope you and Blake are both as happy as I am...Love, Mom.

When Dad died a year and a half later, and the mortuary attendant at Rose Hills Memorial Park in Whittier asked mother to bring clothes in which to bury him, she told me that "...there was no problem in deciding which suit she would choose. He'd want to wear the brown one that he wore at your wedding. That was the proudest day of his life."

Chapter Eleven

"Me And My Shadow"

Dana, my thirteen-year-old son, went into the living room to turn on television. In the kitchen, I was making sure his two younger brothers, Kenny, nine, and Larry, seven, finished the dinner dishes and cleaned up properly. Linda, almost five, was already sitting on her daddy's lap. She was a wiggly little girl, and I knew that after a few minutes of snuggling next to Blake she would slither down to her favorite spot on the carpet to watch television.

"Hurry up, Mom," Dana called, "Ed Sullivan's already on."

"Be right there," I said, told Kenny and Larry they had done a good job, and ushered my young kitchen crew into the living room. Blake sat down next to me on the couch while all four children were on the floor in front of the TV. We had been waiting anxiously all week for this particular Ed Sullivan show.

"Think this'll be a 'really big *shoe*'?" said Dana, my comedian son who mimicked Ed Sullivan by saying "shoe" instead of "show." Kenny and Larry laughed, which put them in good graces with their older brother who loved a responsive audience.

"Okay boys, that's enough," Blake, a serious man, cautioned. "Be quiet, now. Your mother wants you to watch this. You know how she feels about him."

"It's alright, Blake, they're just having fun... Oh, look, Ed Sullivan just announced him. Quiet everyone. Let's watch."

As Ed Sullivan left one end of the stage, a man appeared at the opposite end and was soon followed by another man. Both were dressed in black tuxedos, top hats, and carried canes. Two shadows, the first one taller than the second and displayed on a screen behind them, moved in sync with the two men as they strolled across the stage singing Me and My Shadow.

Television had brought Ted Lewis back into my life.

Chapter Twelve

"A Good Man Is Hard To Find"

Mother answered her phone after the second ring. "Hello," she said, sounding alone, desolate, and rejected.

I'm in for big trouble. I should have called on Monday. "Hi, Mother. Are you feeling better?"

"No, I'm afraid not. My toe is getting worse, I think. Why didn't you call Monday?"

"Mother, I'm really sorry. I promise to come down to Carlsbad on Friday. Okay? Do you think Joe will mind if I take you out to lunch...just the two of us? I have a couple of things to ask you about Ted Lewis." Joe was Mother's fourth husband–three others had died–and I was still not allowed to mention Ted Lewis when in her home. *Will she ever tell me why?*

There was a long silence before she answered, "Ted Lewis?" as if she had never heard of him. Then she became animated and said, "Oh, lunch. I'll see if he minds not going with us and call you back. Ouch! Damn it. I hit that toe again." With a glum and listless "Goodbye, dear," Mother was again the actress martyr facing possible amputation of a perfectly healthy big toe.

At lunch Mother and I sat by the restaurant window watching small boats bob gently up and down in wakes of water as incoming and outgoing boats caused tracks as they motored in and out of the small marina where they docked. We were just finishing our lunch.

"Mother, how much do you know about Ted Lewis?"

Mother kept eating while I let her ponder my question that she seemed not to hear. I was about to ask again when she laid down her fork and looked at me.

"What about Ted Lewis, Dawn," she said sternly.

" I was wondering, do you know if there were any biographies written about him?"

"Oh, yes," she said, seeming more relaxed and at ease. "There was one, I'm sure. Have you looked?"

"Yes, in a few bookstores and libraries. So far I can't find a thing. Do you know the name of the book?"

"I think it was, <u>Is Everybody Happy</u>? She laughed. "What else could it be?"

I asked if she was sure, Mother nodded "yes," and she asked me why I was looking for it.

"We watched one of his old movies the other night, the one with Abbot and Costello–<u>Hold That Ghost</u> it was called–and I got to thinking about a couple of old television interviews with him. One was with Edward R. Murrow. Remember <u>Person to Person</u>? On that one he was really animated and outgoing, like we've always seen him. But, when Ralph Edwards interviewed him on <u>This is Your Life</u>, he was withdrawn, almost silent, the exact opposite of when he's on stage. It was as if there were two different Ted Lewises. Just thought I'd like to read about him, that's all. Thanks, Mother. I'll look for that title."

As we left the restaurant, I noticed Mother resumed her normal quick and graceful walk. Still the showgirl, I thought. *Guess her toe's healed. Joe will be relieved.*

When Blake got home I told him about my mother telling me about a biography.

"Do you think she's right? Blake asked. "You know your mother."

"Can't hurt to look. Want to help? We can start next

Saturday looking through those little bookstores on Hollywood Boulevard. How about your handball game at the Hollywood 'Y' first, and then lunch. Okay?"

After lunch we began our walk on Hollywood Boulevard in search of bookstores. "Larry Edmunds Books" was our first stop.

"I'm sorry," a very helpful clerk said. "I've looked, but we don't have any books at all about Ted Lewis and no record of the title, <u>Is Everybody Happy</u>? If there were such a book we should know about it. But, you probably will want to check at other bookstores in the area, anyway." He sighed as if no one ever believed his information. He gave us names of two other bookstores on Hollywood Boulevard. "There are others, too," he added.

We thanked him and left. Just as we went out the front door I noticed a large star encased in the sidewalk.

"Look, Blake, Gene Autrey's star is right outside their front door." Blake joined me as we both silently read the gold letters honoring this famous western movie star and singer turned baseball entrepreneur for the Los Angeles Angels. Those stars whose names were encased in the sidewalk greeted millions of pedestrians each year as they walked over Hollywood Boulevard's Walk of Fame, the Movie Capital's permanent tribute to its movie, radio, and television celebrities. "Blake, I wonder where Ted Lewis' star is? Let's look for it."

"Do you still think there is any such book as "Is Everybody Happy," Blake said. We were both tired after several hours of fruitless search for a biography about Ted Lewis.

"You're right. I guess it just doesn't exist. You'd think someone would have written something, wouldn't you? I give up."

Blake was unlocking our front door when I said, "There's something else we didn't find."

"What's that?"

"Nothing for Ted Lewis on the Walk of Fame. Now we have two things to look for, a book and a star."

Chapter Thirteen

"Old Playmate"

I am the oldest graduate student ever to be accepted into the Masters Degree program in Journalism at the University of Southern California, Los Angeles.
Have you checked your facts?
No, I haven't.
So, how do you know it's true that you're the oldest?
Well, it feels like it's true.

The three of us, Michael, Louise and I, were early and the first of our twelve member graduate class to arrive at the television lab for our nighttime Broadcast Journalism class. I loved being in this simulated television station with its cameras and monitors, and felt privileged to study with these young, intelligent, vibrant and inquisitive graduate students. Michael and I were talking in the back of the room while Louise was reading in the front. Michael had just asked me where I graduated. The University of California at Berkeley, I told him, and asked him about his school.

"UCLA," he said.

I told him my daughter wanted to go there.

"It's a great school," he added. "Dawn, when did you graduate from Berkeley?"

"Back in the Dark Ages."

"Oh, com'on, it wasn't that long ago." Michael looked at me and said, "How old are you, anyway?"

"Michael, never ask a lady her age. Rule number one for good PR." I sighed and gave in to his question. "Michael, do I really have to tell you my age?" He nodded "yes" and I said, "Let's see how good you are at math. I was born in March of 1929 and this is April of 1982."

Michael became a lightning calculator as he entered computer mode. "You're fifty-three?" he said as other students began coming into the room. "You can't be. Hey, Louise, guess how old Dawn is."

Louise looked back at us, a disinterested spectator. "I don't know. How old is she?"

Some other students joined the quest.

"She's fifty-three," he shouted, making sure Louise could hear this important news.

"Oh, thanks, Michael. Now everyone at USC knows how old I am."

"That means you'll be fifty-four next year when you get your MA. Wow!"

Chapter Fourteen

"Sing a Little Love Song For Your Baby"

Dorothy Parker was on the list of writers I needed to know about for my Masters Degree comprehensive examination in June, at University of Southern California. My favorite "fact" about Miss Parker? When a reporter asked her if she liked to write. Her answer was, "I hate to write, but I love having written." *Right on, girl!*

I was at my desk at home studying for this exam, and scooted down in my chair to get comfortable before adding this "Dorothy Parker" anecdote to my list of things to memorize.

About an hour and three trips to the refrigerator later, the phone rang as I pondered important details regarding another journalist, William Randolph Hearst. I had just crossed off from my list that "He had an affair with Marion Davies, the actress" as being academically irrelevant, although interesting.

"Blake Williams Road Boring," I answered, stating the name of our company.

Silence.

"Hello," I said, hoping my greeting change would provoke a response, but there was still no answer. I started to hang up, then decided to give "hello" one more try.

"Is Dawn Williams there?" said an unfamiliar voice.

"This is she. May I help you?"

The author, Dawn Williams, in 1983.

"Dawn, this is your cousin, Samantha."

"I'm sorry. You must have the wrong 'Dawn.' I don't have any cousin named Samantha. I don't have any cousins at all."

"Oh, I forgot. They used to call me 'Sammy' or 'Sam.' I insisted on Samantha after I got married. You might remember me by Sam."

"I still don't know..."

"I'm your Uncle Robert's step-daughter. Remember? You only saw me two or three times when we were younger and again at my mother's funeral. But, that was a long time ago."

I remembered. "Of course, Sam...Sammy. I used to think that we both had boys' names. Usually people thought my name was 'D-o-n' instead of D-a-w-n," I said, spelling out each name. "Sammy, are you in town?"

"Oh, I live in LA. But, what I called about, well, I need to discuss something with you and thought we might have lunch, next week if you can. Some place close to you?"

"I'd love to have lunch, Sam. And yes, next week would be best for me." I looked down at the jumble of books and papers in front of me and said, "I'll be ready for a break from studying by then. How about meeting you Thursday at the new Buffums in Long Beach? Is noon okay?"

"I know exactly where Buffums is. I'll be there at twelve. And Dawn, I'm really looking forward seeing you. Thursday it is."

"Me too, Sam." After we hung up, I stood looking at the phone a few moments more. *Why did she call? What in the world do we have to discuss? Is it about my uncles? Guess I'll find out Thursday.* I sat down, returned to my "Hearst" list, and decided to leave in "Marion Davies." *A bit of spice never hurts.*

By the time I arrived at Buffums restaurant at noon the following Thursday, Long Beach had tossed aside its early morning gray flannel sky in favor of warm, Southern California sunshine. After the hostess sat me in a booth and asked if someone was joining me for lunch, I told her, yes. "Her name is Samantha," I said, "but I don't know what she looks like. She's probably close to sixty." I told her I would wait to order and she returned to her station where a line of customers was now beginning to form. By twelve-twenty I was still alone and figured Samantha was not going to show up.

"Would you like to order now?" said the waitress as she took out her order book."

"Might as well," I said and started to look at the menu when I decided first to look for Samantha by the restaurant entrance. "Just a minute, I'll be right back. I'm going to see if my friend is out in front."

I walked past the hostess, now standing by a small podium and looking at an open book resting on top. Just then a woman rushed through the entrance, passed me, and ran up to the hostess. They spoke a few words and the hostess, who had seen me pass by her, turned towards me and pointed in my direction. Then the woman came over to me, breathless, and said, "You must be Dawn. I'm Samantha," and grabbed my hand. "I am so sorry to be so late and all I have is a California excuse-the freeway. The 405 was tied up like you would not believe."

I hugged this step cousin whom I still hardly recognized. "You aren't that late, Samantha. Besides, I've been held up by traffic myself a thousand times, only it's usually the 605. Come on. I've got a booth for us."

During lunch our conversation was thin. "How is your mother?" "Do you think George and Robert are happy at the retirement home?" "Robert still misses your mother." "Are your children all married?" Nor did it improve during our coffee and dessert. I doubted, finally, that this stranger really had anything of substance to discuss. *I've got to get back to my studies.*

Finally, Samantha said, "Dawn, there's something I have to tell you." She paused and took a drink of coffee. "I'm afraid I don't know where to begin." She put down her cup and sighed as if the worst part of her mission was over.

64

"Well," I said, trying to put her at ease, "I guess the best thing to do is to begin at the beginning."

Samantha smiled at my effort to be light hearted, but still looked nervous. "Do you think we can get some more coffee?"

Why is she stalling?

The waitress refilled our cups. Samantha drank most of her coffee before continuing. Finally, she said, "This is about your father."

"My father?" I said, puzzled by her statement. "What about my father." *She doesn't even know who my father is.*

"Your father, Dawn, was not Fred Whipple."

"What a terrible thing to say, Samantha, I blurted out without thinking." *How can this person possibly know my father's name? How dare she tell me Fred Whipple was not my father? I can show her his name on my birth certificate.*

"What do you mean Fred Whipple is not my father? You never even met him. He died when I was three."

"I mean just that, Dawn. Fred Whipple is not your father." Samantha seemed irritated that I did not believe her.

Shocked by such an obscene statement, my head seemed void of any logic or ability to answer back. I could not believe what I just heard. Slowly, I regained enough composure and confidence to challenge this blasphemous intrusion into my private life by some woman who was almost a complete stranger.

"Well, Samantha, if he isn't my father, then who is?" I said, indignant and defying her lie about my father. I knew she could not answer this question, and our ridiculous conversation would be over.

Samantha was silent.

"Did you hear me, Samantha?" I said, demanding an answer that I was sure she did not have. "Who is my father?"

"Do you really want to know?" Samantha asked.

"Of course. At least tell me who it is you seem to think he is. We both know that this whole thing is...is a fraud." I was so angry I was grasping for words, and "fraud" was the best I could do.

She said nothing for what seemed an eternity before she continued. "I guess I didn't even think that this might upset you. It certainly was not my intention, and I'm sorry for that. Dawn, I was just thinking about how thrilled you'd be when you found out who your real father was when I told you."

"Oh, really, Samantha? And just how do you think you'd feel if someone you hardly knew told you that your father wasn't your father at all? Let me guess. I think you might be down right livid and walk right out of here...which is exactly the way I feel and what I'm going to do...now." I picked up my purse and started to stand.

"Please, Dawn, let me finish. Then if you still want to leave, well...you're certainly free to go."

Reluctantly, I sat down again. "Okay. Go ahead. Finish. But, first answer my question. If Fred Whipple isn't my father, then who is?"

Again, Samantha said nothing.

"Can't do it, can you, Samantha?"

"Yes, I can," she said vehemently, as if suddenly coming back to life, "and will...right now." Samantha leaned across the table, starred into my eyes for several seconds before she dropped her bomb. "Your father, Dawn, is Ted Lewis."

Chapter Fifteen

"Blues My Naughtie Sweetie Gave To Me"

A detonation caused by a stranger had just ripped apart my life and shattered my past. Simultaneously it triggered in me an explosion of joy that I might possibly be the daughter of Ted Lewis. Does this mean that William Whipple from New Hampshire who signed The Declaration of Independence was not my great great great great Uncle? If I gain a celebrity entertainer as a father, do I lose a Patriot ancestor? How many crazy ideas, I thought, can go through my mind at the same time? Well, Dawn Whipple Williams, or whatever your name is now, it looks like you're about to find out.

"Are you crazy, Samantha...completely out of your mind? I don't know why you are telling me such a lie, but I think our conversation stops here." I snatched the lunch bill from a small brown tray, picked up my purse, and started to slide out of the booth.

Samantha grabbed my hand. "It's not a lie, Dawn. It's the truth. I knew that Ted Lewis was your father before the first time I met you...when we were kids. Please, don't go. Let me explain. Stay."

I jerked my hand out of hers, thought a bit. I sat down. "Alright. But, only while I have another cup of coffee." I was shaking so hard I doubted I could hold the cup. I needed something, anything, to hold on to. My insides were about to explode.

The waitress again filled both cups with fresh, steaming brew, and Samantha was silent until I finished mine. As I put my cup down, I said, "Samantha, this is absolutely insane. I really don't have anything more to say to you and I have to be going."

"First, listen. Hear me out. You may feel differently when I finish."

Resigned to hearing her explanation, I gave in to her request. "Okay, for a few minutes, but I'll still feel this is idiotic," and I settled back ...to hear this fairytale, this lie that defames two fine men.

All of a sudden, something she said made me ask, "What do you mean, you knew about my father before you met me?"

"Remember when your uncle married my mother? Well, you were only about eight or nine and hadn't met me yet, but I heard a lot about you. You know your Uncle Robert loved you like a daughter. Sometimes I even felt a little jealous. He never thought of me as his child. After all, I was almost fourteen when they married and was away at Catholic boarding school."

"He's been like a father to me." I felt more relaxed as we talked about my favorite uncle.

"After they got married we celebrated at the Biltmore Bowl where Ted Lewis was entertaining. Remember, I had no idea about who Ted Lewis was until I heard my mother and Robert whispering. I asked my mother what they were talking about. She said, Ted Lewis, the man on the stage leading the band, and she'd tell me about him when we got home.

"This was the first stage show I ever saw and was pretty bored, until I heard about this secret. After that I paid more attention to Ted Lewis, even sort of liked what he did. Especially the part where he sings about a shadow. I remember him doing tricks with a beat up looking hat and getting all sorts of shouts and applause when he said, 'Is everybody happy?' The audience sure did love him."

"You mean, Samantha, you never even heard of Ted Lewis? I thought everyone had."

"Remember, Dawn, music and stage shows were not part of my life. We probably didn't see more than two...if that...movies a year." I nodded and said that I understood, but it was hard for me to imagine this void.

"When we got home my mother first told me what a famous man Ted Lewis was, and that he was popular all over the world. Then she said that whatever else she told me that 'Dawn must never find out' and that I wasn't to repeat any of this to anyone, even Robert, and especially your mother. Then she said, 'Ted Lewis is Dawn's real father.' When I asked her if anyone else knew, she said, 'Yes, everyone in the whole family knows, except Dawn, and she must never know.' When I asked her why, she just said, 'I don't know why, but that's the way it is,' and made me promise again never to tell. I guess Mother was dying to tell someone and she knew I'd keep a secret."

Again, something that Samantha said triggered another question. Everyone knew but me? My entire family knew? I can understand Mother keeping this a secret. But, Grandma? She would never hide something like this from me. Never. "This is even harder to believe, Samantha, than your tale about Ted Lewis being my father."

"Yes, everyone. They all talked about it when you weren't around. Of course, I had to be quiet because I wasn't supposed to know."

"Even if this preposterous story were true, and it isn't, Samantha, it can't possibly be, why are you telling me this now. After all these years?"

"Because of your uncles, especially George."

"What about Uncle George. Is he Okay?" He was in his early nineties, and I was concerned about his health, although he seemed well the last time I saw him.

"He feels okay, but he's very disturbed, actually quite upset. I went to see him last month and couldn't believe what I saw in his room. There were little pieces of paper everywhere, on tables, pinned to the drapes, scotch taped to the refrigerator and furniture, even on a lampshade and the bathtub. On each piece of paper he had written either 'Ted Lewis' or 'Dawn' or both. When I asked him why he did this, he said, 'I'm afraid all of us are going to die, and Dawn will never know that her real father is Ted Lewis. I have to tell her while I'm still here.' That's when I knew you had to hear it from me."

"One more thing, Dawn, I brought this for you. It's yours to keep if you like." Samantha reached into an oversize purse and brought out a small folder. She opened it and handed it to me.

Inside was a photograph of several people. They were seated at a large table with a stage in the background. I recognized my Uncle Robert, his wife, and Sam as a teenager. The others I did not know. All looked very young.

"That was taken at the wedding celebration for Mother and Robert at the Builtmore Bowl. Robert told me that the dinner and show were a gift from some man he used to be chauffeur for."

"Barron Long," I said. "He owned the Biltmore, I think, and Uncle Robert used to be his driver when he was in town."

"That's his name. What a memory you have."

I smiled, thinking of another time concerning Ted Lewis that my grandmother questioned my memory. As I thought of her and how close we were, I was sure she would have told me. I was now absolutely sure Samantha was wrong. *Absolutely, Dawn? Isn't there still a tiny itch of doubt?*

"I will keep this picture, Samantha, and thank you for giving it to me." I picked up my purse, the bill, and stood up. "Lunch is on me. I have a lot to think about. I hope you understand that I can never believe this story is true, but I do thank you for coming. Friends?" I held out my hand and she shook it.

"Friends. If it was me, I guess I might feel the same. Thanks, anyway, for listening, and for lunch." As she left the table she turned to me and said, "It's true, Dawn, all of it. I guess you'll just have to find out for yourself."

We left Buffums separately. Sam was gone from my life as quickly as she entered.

I was left alone to think about the unbelievable.

Chapter Sixteen

"I'm Walking Around in a Dream"

The sound of my slamming car door jarred many of my frantic senses as I prepared to leave Buffums. *Oh, dear God, I've got to find Blake and tell him what I just heard.*

Those few miles I drove to the Long Beach Athletic Club where I knew Blake was playing handball seemed surreal. The reality of the road I traveled daily, became fantasy, passing traffic became a bizarre dream of silent automobiles rushing towards nowhere, while I sat in the drivers seat with my hands on a steering wheel where I controlled...nothing. I was a phantom driver driving a phantom car on a phantom street. Oblivious to all reality around me, I somehow arrived at my club, the comfort of its familiar sight bringing me back from the living dead.

Now somewhat recovered, I was glad to see Angie, the club's receptionist, was at the front desk. Her familiar face forced my mind away from those alien thoughts that invaded my brain during the past hours.

"Angie, please page Blake for me." I collapsed onto a black leather visitor's couch.

"You sure, Dawn? He's not going to be happy to leave his game. Dawn, are you okay?"

"That's an understatement. Furious is more like it. Yes, Angie, I'm fine. I have to see him, Angie."

"Okay, but I'm going to hide under this desk while he throws handballs around the club." We both laughed at this image. I was feeling a little more at ease.

After a long five minutes, Blake walked towards me, obviously upset that he had to leave the court. *What's he going to think when I tell him?*

"It's what you think, that matters," said Blake after hearing Samantha's Ted Lewis fable.

"Blake, I don't know what, or even how, to think. Right now I don't know if I can think at all. I just had to see you, and tell you."

"Do you believe her?"

"Of course not. How can you even ask?"

"You know that dream world your mother lives in. It's possible the story's true and she was never going to tell you." Blake patted me on the shoulder and said, "Let's talk about it tonight. I have to get back to my game. Are you okay?"

"Yes, well, not exactly okay, but I'll make it home. Let's go out to dinner."

"Sure. See you tonight, and I'm glad you told me."

Driving home I allowed myself to think about what Blake had said...*it's possible the story's true*...but discarded this improbable claim. No. No, I said out loud. It's a lie. My mother would never keep something like this from me.

Don't be so sure, Dawn. Think about it.

At dinner I did most of the talking. Blake wanted to hear every detail of my lunch with Samantha. Only two or three times did he interrupt to ask a question. It was eleven o'clock when we got home from dinner and went to bed.

Her story still boggled my mind and kept me awake. No rest tonight, I thought, and went into the living room and sat on the couch.

"What are you doing in here?" said Blake as he came into the living room. "It's only two o'clock."

"Trying to figure things out," I said.

Blake said nothing, but sat on the couch next to me.

"Why did she have to tell me this? I want my life back, Blake."

"You just need a few days to think about what you're going to do and it'll be fine. Come on back to bed, now." He took my hand and we returned to our room.

By the end of the following week my confusion yielded to clarity. "Blake," I said one night, I've come to a decision."

"You mean about Ted Lewis?"

"Yes." Both of us had been silent about Samantha and Ted Lewis since she told me her story.

"Good. It's about time. What is it?"

"I'm going to find out the truth."

Chapter Seventeen

"Somebody Stole My Gal"

We enjoyed an hour and thirty minutes of easy driving on an almost barren freeway - light traffic is a rare luxury on a Southern California Sunday - before Blake and I arrived at my mother's home in Carlsbad. I expected hell after we got there and I was not disappointed. I was, however, surprised and unprepared for the form hell would take when I confronted my mother concerning the truth about my father.

***

"And how are you going to do that," Blake asked after I had told him my decision to resolve this improbable claim that Ted Lewis was my father. I answered him by explaining the details of my plan that featured my mother and her two brothers.

"I'm going to take each of my two uncles, then my mother, to lunch separately and then ask each one about my father when we're alone. It's simple and direct. Besides, they're the only people still living who would know the answer. What do you think?"

"Well, good luck. Oh, your uncles you won't have a problem with, but your mother might be something else. If this thing is true, just think. She'd kept this a secret all these years and I don't think she's going to want to give it up. If it's not true, she might have had something to do with this rumor getting started.

She's not going to like it either way."

"That's why I have to talk to each one alone, and keep my questions simple and objective. I don't want to influence their answers. So, how does this sound. First, I'm not going to tell them why I'm taking them to lunch. Then, when the time is right, I'm going to ask them two questions. The first one is, 'Was Fred Whipple my father?' If they say 'Yes' I won't need the second question. If it is 'No,' my next and final question is, 'Who is?'"

"What if each one gives a different answer?"

"I'll figure out what to do about that later."

"Well, sounds like a good plan to me. What's most important is you're not influencing what they say."

"Exactly what I intended," I said smiling, then became serious. "My uncles will be great, however they answer. Blake, I'm not looking forward to confronting my mother. I just don't know what to expect."

***

When Uncle George got out of the elevator and saw me in the lobby of the retirement home in Long Beach where he and Uncle Robert occupied separate apartments, he grinned and gave me a hug. At ninety-one his frame was still tall, thin, and angular as if food had evaded him all his life. Below his straight and sparse hair, more brown than gray, protruded a large prominent nose. We exchanged a few "hellos" and "what's happening?" before getting into my car and driving to Hofs Hut for lunch a few miles away. This was the first time we were ever together alone.

After lunch I decided it was time to ask my questions. I was nervous, but tried to look calm.

"Uncle George," I said. I kept my hands under the table because they were shaking, "I have something to ask you. Please, promise to tell me the truth, no matter what."

Uncle George put the coffee cup back on its saucer and

removed his long, spike fingers from its handle. "Of course, Dawn, you can ask me anything, especially after that wonderful pie and ice cream." He grinned, laughed a little, then took another drink of his coffee.

"The truth, you promise?"

"Dawn, of course I'll tell you the truth, whatever it is.

"Well, Uncle George, it's about my father."

He stopped drinking his coffee, stared at me, and clutched his cup with those bony hands as if it were his lifeline. He was silent, as if afraid to speak. *He knows.*

I gave him another few seconds to digest my statement, then began my questions. "Uncle George," I said and drew a deep breath before I continued. "Was my father Fred Whipple?"

I looked at his face, already ashen with age, now turned deadly white as he sat silently. His eyes filled with tears which flooded down deep ravines etched in his face. I handed him one of the several tissues I brought for myself, and was glad I had one for him. For an eternity we sat looking at each other before he answered.

"No. No, Dawn, he wasn't."

"Who was?" I asked, but wanted to say, "Stop. I don't want to hear the rest."

Quickly he said, "Ted Lewis," as if he could hardly wait to rid himself of this reply, this secret, he had carried for so many years.

We drank our coffee in silence for several minutes and the warm liquid stroked my shattered senses. *Why do crises always call for coffee?* I started to continue, but he spoke first.

"It's the truth, Dawn. I feel like the world is off my shoulders. Some one should have told you a long time ago." Then he smiled and said, "I'm glad you finally know."

"Thank you, Uncle George, for telling me." I still was not convinced. "How did you know about all this?" Despite his affirmation that my father was Ted Lewis, it still seemed unbelievable. *He has to be wrong.*

Uncle George seemed relieved and was now more animated. "Dawn," he said, "we all knew. Your mother couldn't keep quiet about it. You know her. She'd have to tell somebody, everybody. Well, she told everyone she knew that she was expecting a baby and made no bones about it being Ted Lewis' child. We all knew Fred Whipple had been on a business trip for several months and couldn't be the father. Then, after you were born, she said we were not to tell anyone about Ted Lewis, that you would be brought up as Fred Whipple's daughter. Ted Lewis is your father, Dawn."

As I drove up in front of the retirement home a few days later, Uncle Robert was waiting for me at the curb.

"Hofs Hut, Uncle Robert?" I said as he closed the car door and settled himself into the passenger seat.

"Where else is there?" He laughed, and leaned over to kiss my cheek before he fastened his seat belt. "Let's go." My uncle, always happy, was tall, slim, and still handsome at eighty-eight, with only slight gray touches in his dark brown hair.

"No dessert for me, Dawn," Uncle Robert said after finishing lunch. Several senior women at a table nearby kept looking over at my uncle and giggling as if they were schoolgirls. *Sorry, ladies, he's with me.*

Both Uncle Robert and I had been quietly drinking our coffee which the waitress occasionally refilled. She seemed to sense we were homesteading our booth a while longer. Finally I said, "Uncle Robert, I have something to ask you. Okay?"

"Sure. Ask away. I'll tell my favorite niece anything I know."

"This is pretty important, Uncle Robert, and I have to have the truth. Promise me you'll tell me the truth?"

"Of course you'll get the truth. Why so serious, and why would I ever not tell you the truth?" Fire away, honey. I'll tell you anything I can." He grinned and settled into the corner of our booth.

"It's about my father, Uncle Robert."

"Fred Whipple?" He looked puzzled. "A fine man, and a gentleman. Always gave your mother everything she wanted. Too bad he couldn't have lived longer so you two could have known each other."

"Not that. It's something else." I paused, putting off my question to him. Finally I asked, " Uncle Robert, is Fred Whipple my father?"

He took my hands in his. "What makes you ask a question like that, Sweetheart. I don't understand."

"Please, you have to tell me the truth. I know you know and I have to know."

His smile vanished as he leaned forward and kissed both of my hands, then sighed. "Yes, you do need to know. I just never thought I'd be the one to tell you." He was silent while he just looked at me for the longest while.

"Was Fred Whipple my father?" I repeated.

"No, Dawn, Fred Whipple was not your father." He seemed more at ease with this answer than Uncle George did.

"Who was?"

"You already know the answer, don't you, Dawn?" He paused a long time before he continued. "You already know that your father is Ted Lewis. Right?"

We sat there holding hands across the table and not speaking until the waitress asked us if we wanted anything else.

"I guess we'd better go and let someone else sit here," I said, evading an answer to his question. Uncle Robert agreed and we left.

"I need to know how you found out that it was Ted Lewis," I said as I parked at the retirement home curb.

"Honey, I'm going to tell you all about it. I promise. Can we leave that for another day? This is a shock, for both of us, and we've got a lot to think about."

"Sure," I said, then kissed him goodbye as he got out of the car. "Soon?"

"You bet, Dawn." Call me in a few days and we'll talk. I've got a lot to tell you." Before he shut the car door he asked, "Does your mother know about this?"

"No, not yet. Please don't say anything to her."

"I won't. Is this why you took George to lunch last week?"

I nodded, yes.

"He kept your secret just fine. Never said a word." He closed the car door and disappeared into the building.

Well, two down and one to go. So far these two answers are not what I wanted or expected. Why did a tiny voice keep whispering, *Are you sure?*

***

"Hey, Blake, that's a great idea." Joe had finished his pot roast dinner and was waiting to order dessert. "Ruth and I would love the drive to La Jolla to see your work. Right, Ruth?"

"Oh, no, Joe," I said before my mother could answer, "Mother and I will stay and watch TV. I see enough pipelines being put in during the week. Besides, you and Blake will be free to talk "guy" stuff."

"Oh, I don't know..."

"Com'on, Joe," Blake interrupted, not giving Joe a chance to object, "this way we might stop for a beer on the way back. It's all decided, ladies. We'll let you off at the house."

Outnumbered, Joe did not answer and seemed miffed by Blake's interference. He was silent until he said goodbye to my mother and handed her the house key reluctantly as if she were incapable of unlocking a door. Without giving Joe time to object again, Blake drove off quickly before Mother could open the front door.

"I didn't think Blake drank," Mother said as we walked into the house."

"He doesn't," I said.

"Then why'd he offer to buy Joe a beer?"

Ignoring her question, I said, "Take your coat off, Mother, and sit down. I'll explain it all later."

Mother smiled and said, "It sounds mysterious," as she took her coat and purse into the bedroom, then returned and sat down in her chair. "There, I'm sitting. Now what?"

I was still standing when I said, "Mother there's something I have to ask you." I sat down on the matching floral upholstered ottoman in front of her chair.

"Yes?" Mother, at 83, answered with an innocence of youth, a ploy she sometimes used ingeniously to hide the fact that she was actually a very smart and intelligent adult playing the role of ingenue.

I don't think I can do this.

"Dawn, what's this all about?"

"Mother, I have to ask you something and you have to promise me you'll tell me the truth." Mother's idea of truth had always been somewhere between Make-believe and Let's Pretend. I had to convince her that this was time for reality.

"Well?"

"The truth, Mother. You promise?"

"I can't think of any reason not to tell you the truth. What is it?"

"First, promise...the truth."

"Yes, yes, I promise to tell you the truth." Mother seemed annoyed. "There, now, what are you going to ask me?"

Now it was time for me also to face reality. Quickly, before I could retreat, I said, "Mother, was Fred Whipple my father?"

My mother stared at me and sat silently as if unable to speak, her body ridged as it bent slightly toward me, her fingers digging into the soft arm of her chair. I waited for her answer, wanting her to tell me, but at the same time hoping I'd never hear it. "Mother, please, I need to know, now."

"Dawn, did I tell you Joe and I are going to the races in Tijuana next weekend?"

"Mother, you didn't tell me, and that's not what you need to tell me now. Please, answer my question. Is Fred Whipple my father?"

Irritated and glaring at me, Mother answered quickly. "No, Dawn, Fred Whipple is not your father." She gave up this information as if giving away her last breath.

I waited before I asked my next question, as if time could erase the answer I dreaded to hear.

"If Fred Whipple was not my father, then who was, Mother?"

She still kept her silence. Finally, her eyes flooded from uncontrolled tears, and between sobs of anguish, she answered in staccato whispers I could not hear.

"Mother," I said, "I can't understand you. Please try to stop crying. I need to know what you are saying."

As my mother finally held back her tears, she looked at me, her eyes now red and moist, then glanced quickly away as if she were talking to the wall. Somewhat recovered, she looked toward the other end of the room, and began to speak clearly enough that I could understand her still muffled answer. But, there was no doubt as to what she said. "Your father, Dawn," Mother repeated, "is...Ted Lewis."

Chapter Eightteen

"Where'd You Get Those Eyes"

When Joe and Blake returned from La Jolla, they found my mother ill and in bed.

"What happened, Dawn?" Joe said to me as we both stood next to my mother. He sat down on the edge of the bed, feeling my mother's forehead with the back of his hand. "Ruth, are you all right?" He leaned closer to her ear. "Do you want a doctor?"

Mother opened her eyes, groaned when she saw Joe, then closed them as she returned to a fitful half-sleep. I motioned both Blake and Joe to follow me out of the room.

"I think she's okay, Joe. Just got sick to her stomach. Let her sleep. Must have been something she ate at dinner." I lied. The truth was that after Mother said, "Ted Lewis," she jumped up from her chair, ran into the bathroom, and threw up several times. Then I put her to bed where Joe found her when he and Blake returned. "Don't worry, Joe," I said, "she'll be okay."

Blake and I stayed another hour to make sure my mother was sleeping soundly before we left. "Tell Mother I'll call her in the morning, Joe, and I'll call you when we get home. Just to be sure she's alright."

Neither Blake nor I spoke until we got onto the freeway.

"Well?" said Blake, breaking the silence.

"Give me a couple of minutes. I'm not sure how to think

about what just happened."

At Oceanside Blake interrupted my thoughts. "I can't wait any longer. What happened?"

"Blake, you may not be married to the girl you think you are married to. I'm not even sure I'm who I think I am."

Blake paused, then said, "Does that mean she said Ted Lewis is your father?"

"Yes. That's when she threw up...after she told me." The rest of the way home I told Blake every detail of the past hours.

"Well," said Blake after I finished, "at least we're sure of one thing. Your first name is Dawn." We laughed at this weak joke, grasping for anything to remove the tension created by my mother's revelation that I was, indeed, the daughter and only child of Ted Lewis, "The Jazz King."

By Wednesday I had come to grips with this fact that Ted Lewis was my father. Still, I was reluctant to admit that I was his daughter. The title was too new, still so improbable. On one hand, I hoped something, or someone, would prove this all a hoax so my life could return to normal. On the other hand, I glowed in the knowledge that Ted Lewis could possibly be my father.

Does this make me someone else? No, I answered myself out loud when I was alone. I am the same "me." *Do I feel differently as the daughter of Ted Lewis than I did as Fred Whipple's child?* Absolutely. I have a sense of joy, an euphoria that I never felt before as Fred Whipple's daughter. I feel all these feelings at once in knowing that I am Ted Lewis' child. *Do I know what to do with this knowledge about my parents?* Not a clue, I thought. But, one thing I'm sure of. Whatever her reason for keeping this from me, I know my mother thought she was doing right and did the very best she could. I could not fault her or feel anger towards her. I loved my mother. *Do I wish she had told me so I could have known him?* Oh, yes.

When I called Uncle Robert that afternoon, I told him

everything about my conversation with her.

"Honey, I'm glad she finally told you the truth," he said. "It must have been hard for her. Can you come over tomorrow, Dawn, and I'll tell you the rest of my own story."

"Get comfy, Sweetheart," Uncle Robert said the next day after I arrived at his apartment, "this will take some time."

I sat down in his threadbare mohair chair, placed next to a matching couch where he now sat. I snuggled into the impression molded by time under the weight of Uncle Robert's body until I felt comfortable. It's a perfect fit, I thought, and smiled as I wondered if Uncle Robert had me in mind each time he sat in this chair, and formed this depression just for me. Then, as he related in detail his involvement in this seemingly never-ending saga...this mystery...about Ted Lewis, my family, and me, I felt like a jury of one hearing a final witness testify at a trial to determine who my father really was.

"George told me he told you that your mother told everyone she knew, friends and family. That's true. Ruth just couldn't keep quiet about being pregnant with Ted Lewis' child... you know how your mother loves celebrity. Everyone had to know. This was too exciting to keep to herself. Fred Whipple was gone on a business trip to the East Coast for months when she announced that she was 'expecting.' We all knew the father couldn't be Fred. Usually your mother went with him on these long trips. But this time she stayed home. So, we all believed her... no matter how insane it sounded... when she said that Ted Lewis was the father. No reason not to.

"By the time he...Fred... got back, she was already beginning to show. And we all wondered what she was going to tell him. But, Honey, your mother will have to tell you about that. She sort of froze up about the subject after Fred came home.

"I got more involved in this a few months before you were born. Fred called me one day and asked me to come to their apartment in Hollywood. When I got there he explained that a lawyer for Ted Lewis was coming to their home in about an hour and wanted me to witness some papers he and Ruth had to sign. It seems that Ted Lewis had agreed to pay them ten thousand dollars to keep quiet about Ted Lewis being your father. Boy, if his fans knew about him and your mother in those days, why his career wouldn't have been worth the powder to blow it up. It would have ruined his whole life if the public knew about them and you.

"Anyway, the lawyer was bringing half of the money, five thousand dollars that day, and then the other five thousand after you were born. The money was to be kept for your education. You mother said Ted Lewis was adamant about that in the contract. So, they needed me both times as a witness. Also, the lawyer was supposed to see you before he turned over the rest of the money. Ted Lewis and his wife wanted him to see what you looked like, I guess, if he thought you could possibly be Ted's child.

"Now remember, Dawn, ten thousand dollars was a huge sum back in 1929. Fred Whipple was ecstatic. He had lost just about all his money in bad investments. And to boot, he was not used to being poor."

"A lot of good that money did Mother and me," I interrupted. "Fred Whipple spent it all to get himself out of trouble. Look how poor Mother was after he died. Didn't have enough money to bury him. She couldn't even afford to keep me. Remember visiting me in that orphanage?"

"I sure do. It broke my heart to see you there. But let me finish.

"So, I went to their apartment both times the same lawyer came. Each time I signed some papers, and afterwards waited in the hall 'till he left. I didn't read either one. Just signed. What was interesting was when he came the second time, after you were born. He took one look at you and said, 'Oh, yes. Look at those eyes.' You looked like Ted even then, Dawn."

Blake teases me about having bullfrog eyes and being chinless. I always thought Blake's comments about my large eyes and slightly receding chin, were his idea of humor and I never took them seriously. Now his words took on a new meaning for me. *At last I look like someone I'm related to.*

"That night Fred took your mother and me out to dinner at Musso Franks on Hollywood Boulevard. He said it was to celebrate the ten thousand dollars that was going to get him out of a whole lot of trouble. They left you with your nanny, and the three of us had a great time. I'd never seen Fred so happy."

Blake was already home when I got back from hearing what Uncle Robert had to tell me.

"Could we go to Musso Franks for dinner tonight?" I asked, explaining why I wanted to be there when I told him Uncle Robert's story.

"Sure. Where is it?" Neither of us had been there before.

"On Hollywood Boulevard, just west of the Pantages Theater." The Pantages was an elaborate and ornate movie theater that opened in 1928, and now hosted stage shows and musicals. It was one of our favorite theaters. "A lot of celebrities go to Mussos."

We arrived early at Mussos and were seated immediately by a formally attired waiter who took us to one of the private, high-backed booths made of dark, rich wood. After we ordered, I began telling Blake Uncle Robert's story before the salad arrived, and finished during dessert.

"I can see why you wanted to be here to tell me," Blake said. "Being where it happened makes your story come alive."

"And real," I added, imagining those three adults and their dinner celebration, perhaps in this very booth, which culminated in the events that would determine the direction of the rest of my life.

Chapter Nineteen

"My Little Girl"

The day after our dinner at Musso's, Blake asked me if I was going to tell the children that Ted Lewis was my father. "Or are you going to keep it a secret...just between us?"

"Absolutely no," I said. "This lie ends here. They have a right to know who their grandfather is."

When Linda called that afternoon, I asked her to come over the next day. "Your father and I have something to tell you."

"Sure," she said, "I can be there after class, about noon. Don't forget lunch."

"Perfect," I replied, happy that my request worked in with her demanding schedule at UCLA.

As I hung up the phone, I wondered what you serve your daughter for lunch when you are about to tell her that Ted Lewis is her grandfather? "Surprise Casserole" seemed in order.

Blake and I were both in the kitchen when she arrived.

"Hi. Anyone home?" Linda walked through the entry way and into the kitchen. "Hi, Dad. Where's...Oh, hi, Mom."

I was standing at the sink. The minute I saw her I threw my arms around her and said, "Oh Linda, there's something you need to know."

"Mom, what's wrong? Dad has someone been hurt? Are the boys okay?"

"Everyone's fine," said Blake as he put his arm around her. "Your mother has upsetting news to deal with. That's why we asked you to come over. Linda, it seems your grandmother was fooling around."

Both Linda and I stared at Blake, startled at this comment about his mother-in-law. He was now laughing at one of his infrequent jokes. Linda did not know what he was talking about, and I started laughing along with him, more for relief than a reaction to his wit. I was grateful for the light touch given to what had become at times a burden during the past few weeks.

"Dad, is this about Grandma? What do you mean she was 'fooling around?' She's too old."

"Well, Linda," I said, "she may be too old now, but she sure wasn't too old in 1928."

Chapter Twenty

"She's Funny That Way"

*O**kay. So my life is turned upside-down...and inside out. Is this a "new me" now that I'm not a way-down-the-line niece of a man who signed The Declaration of Independence? Suddenly, Fred Whipple is not my father. And, it does look like I'm the daughter of Ted Lewis...his only child, to boot. Well, Grandma, you knew all the time. Right? Every time you played <u>Me and My Shadow</u> for me on the piano, didn't you?* Heady stuff to think about.

Up to now I allowed myself to plan ahead only so far as to tell my children about their "new grandfather," and to digest the events of the past few weeks.

Linda listened to me tell her these details during lunch at our home. After the part where Samantha told me that Fred Whipple was not my father, she said nothing until I told her that Samantha said my father was Ted Lewis.

"Who?" said Linda.

"Ted Lewis," I repeated.

"Our Ted Lewis?"

"Yes, Linda, *our* Ted Lewis."

"Ted Lewis is your father? Oh, com'on, Mom. Get real."

Blake broke his silence. "Your mother's sure, Linda. Listen to her."

Linda just looked at me until I finished my story. She

looked serious and puzzled.

"You mean, William Whipple with all the 'greats' in front of his name is not my uncle," she said when I finished, "and the real Ted Lewis is my grandfather?"

"Yes, Linda, that's right. Fred Whipple is on my birth certificate as my legal father, but Ted Lewis would be my biological father."

"Incredible," she said, and broke into a smile so broad I thought her face would split. "Save my pie and cut a piece for Melanie. I'm bringing her back with me after I tell her who my new granddad is."

Linda started out the door, stopped, then turned back toward us.

"Oh, my God, Mom, does this mean we're Jewish?"

"I hadn't thought much about it. But, Ted Lewis was Jewish, so...I guess we are. A bit, anyway."

Linda started to laugh. "See, Dad, all your worry for nothing about David's parents not wanting him to go out with me because I'm not Jewish...like them. Now I am. Be right back," she said, and went out the door.

After three other luncheons later, Dana, Kenny and Larry was each told separately, Ted Lewis was my father, and could hardly wait to get out of the house to share this news with their friends.

After telling all my children the truth, seeing their reactions, I was relieved and happy, that night enjoying my first uninterrupted sleep since meeting with Samantha. When I awoke in the morning I felt ready to face my challenge, what do I do now? My answer was, *Right now I have no idea, but I will...soon.*

Is this what floating on cloud nine feels like, I asked myself, glowing inside, conscious of my new heritage? Like my children, I wanted to tell somebody, everybody, who my father was. But, I had something to do first. I needed to get notarized affidavits before a lawyer from my mother and two uncles, detailed accounts of what each had told me. Each one, especially my uncles, seemed eager to shed this family secret they carried for so many years. "We're the only relatives left," said Uncle Robert, "who know your story, Dawn, and we won't be around too much longer to tell about it. George and I feel like we're giving you a gift you should have had a long time ago."

Finally, I felt free to tell my friends. Millie was first to know.

"Mil," I said when she answered her phone, "glad you're home." A good friend since we moved to Seal Beach in 1963, Millie lived in Huntington Harbor, a beautiful and exclusive residential area on the water near Seal Beach. "I'll be right over. I've got something to tell you."

Millie did not take her eyes off me throughout my story and hugged me when it was over. "Ted Lewis. Imagine." She hugged me again, stopped smiling, and looked me in the eye. " I'll never forgive your mother for not telling you."

When I went to tell Sally, I showed her an autographed photo of Ted Lewis with his hat in one hand and his clarinet in another that I bought in one of the Hollywood's bookstores. "Oh yes," she said. There's no doubt. Just look at you two. Dawn, You've always looked just like him." As she handed the picture back to me, we both laughed when she said, "No wonder you didn't drop your cane when we did Me and My Shadow."

My friend, Janet, hung on every word I told her. After a few silent seconds when I finished, she said, "Who's Ted Lewis?"

Last to know was my feature writing professor at USC. "Dawn," he said after hearing that Ted Lewis was my father, "you have a compelling story to tell. You must write a book."

Thank you, that's exactly what I wanted to hear.

Chapter Twenty-One

"I'm Stepping Out With a Memory Tonight"

Wilshire Boulevard displayed its usual noontime traffic overload, living up to its reputation as the most horrible place in the United States to drive during lunch hour. Several green signal lights ahead dared motorists to drive forward, but was ignored by cars backed up for several blocks each way. Their tease caused a stop and go traffic to endure this sluggish pace to both east and west bound motorists, now inching forward only when the red lights ahead of them signaled a deceptive "Halt."

So what? I thought. I'm in no hurry. Besides, it's easier to find the Academy going so slow. In less than a minute, I saw the building in the next block. At the corner I pulled suddenly left, cutting off the advance of several motorists, irate at having to sit through another green light, and honking in rebuff to my unwelcome intrusion. I parked on this side street, walked a few feet to Wilshire and the front entrance to my destination.

In January of 1984, The Academy of Motion Pictures Arts and Sciences Margaret Herrick Library hid upstairs in a small section of its host and namesake, the Academy of Motion Pictures Arts and Sciences building which I just entered. Standing as protector and distributor of Hollywood's movie industry history, I was told that it includes almost everything you want to know about the Charlie Chaplins, the Mary Pickfords, the Tom

Hanks, and Stephen Spielbergs, all those who began, developed, or performed an art form destined to permeate the world. At this library I hoped to begin my search for the life of Ted Lewis.

I knew Ted Lewis' movie career began in 1928 when he first arrived in Hollywood. "It was in June," Mother often told me, "that he came to Hollywood to make movies. I remember going to see him at the Palace Theater where he was appearing with his show just a few days after he arrived." I always assumed she went to this performance with Fred Whipple. However, "Fred was away at the time," she confessed after revealing the true story about my father, "and I went alone." The Academy library, I thought, was the logical place to start my search for the father I never knew, and a logical research source for the biography I would someday write.

"Oh, I'm sorry," a friendly voice said as I stepped from the elevator onto the second floor, "but we require you to check all your belongings before you enter the library." A lady motioned me toward her and showed me a small locker in which to place my purse before I entered the library area. "Security, you know."

I went inside. "How may I help you?" asked an attractive young brunette behind the counter. "Can I get something for you? Is there a certain celebrity you're looking for?

"Yes," I finally said, recovering from my few seconds of amnesia. "Ted Lewis. Do you have any information on Ted Lewis?"

"Ted Lewis?" Let me see, now. Just give me a few minutes to look in our files back here. Be right back."

She returned in a few minutes with two envelopes. "One is filled with clippings—newspapers, magazines, and other stuff— the other has photos. You can sign these out and take them over to one of those tables. Bring them back here when you're finished. Oh, you can copy any of these over there," she said, pointing to a large photocopier, "but, nothing in the folders can leave the library."

"I can't thank you enough," I said. "I didn't expect to find so much." Carrying my two full envelopes like retrieved buried treasure, I went to the nearest vacancy at a table and sat down to begin the biggest adventure of my life. Not only was I going to find out something about Ted Lewis, my favorite entertainer, but at the same time become acquainted with my father.

For several minutes I stared at the closed envelopes, afraid of what I might discover. I had no idea what my library search would reveal. *Only one way to find out, Dawn. Pick one of these envelopes and open it.* I choose the one with clippings, then gently tipped the envelope and carefully urged its contents onto the table with my free hand.

At first I saw only a pool of black and white as newsprint from the envelopes now rested upon the table in a jumbled pile. As I gently, almost reverently, separated one from the other, the pool began to disappear as each item took on its own character and message. Some had photographs. Ted Lewis, 81, Dies In Sleep At Home, illustrated by an aging Ted Lewis wearing his battered hat. WHERE ARE THEY NOW? It was a feature article from Newsweek and contrasted his age in two photos of Ted Lewis, both with his famous hat: one in 1970, the other in 1935. In 1928, the year he came to Hollywood to make one of the first talking movies, was a photo of a young Ted Lewis holding his hat in his right hand and his clarinet in his left. This illustration was for a Los Angeles Times article, Ted Lewis Story' Hotly on Fire Now... written by Edwin Schallert. Other articles were printed without photos: Where's the Melody? Ted Lewis Counterpoint To Today's Tune Styles in Variety; The Los Angeles Herald Examiner featured a United Press International (UPI) story from New York with, THEY THINK I'M TOO CORNY over the main headline, and underneath was written, Unemployed Ted Lewis Seeks Job. Loose photos from the other envelope, both portraits and pictures of his band and entertainers also poured onto the table.

I decided to make copies of both clippings and photos and return home rather than study them at the library. First I copied the clippings, then the photos which I only glanced at quickly as I laid them down on the copier's glass. I noticed that they included head shots of Ted Lewis wearing his top hat, a picture in army uniform with his band, and another photo with his band that   included several stunning showgirls. There were others that I would take more time to look at later.

"There's more material here than I expected," I said when I got home that night. Blake wanted to know what I found out at the Academy. "Look at all this. Blake, with everything I already have, I think I've got a good start on that book."

"Oh, I almost forgot. There's a "Ted Lewis Museum in his hometown." A little place back in Ohio...Circleville. Think how much I can find back there? Blake, can we go to Circleville... soon?"

Chapter Twenty-Two

"Memory Land"

During my research, I had found a copy of an old Ralph Edwards <u>This is Your Life</u> television show that I had seen years before, and sat down to watch it.

As soon as Ralph Edwards, the host, greeted his television audience with, "Good evening, ladies and gentlemen," TV cameras pulled away from these studio spectators and focused on a spotlight now illuminating an old battered top hat and cane.

"There are," he said, "in the entertainment industry today, some people with a rare inner magic that completely bewitches an audience. Tonight's principle subject has so much of this quality of enchantment, so much personality, that for forty years he's been a headliner. There he is, in a studio rehearsing one of the numbers that's become his trademark, his interpretation of <u>Me and My Shadow</u>. To many, many millions of you, this has been a familiar and captivating sight. Now, let's go in and surprise this well-known entertainer."

As Ted Lewis and his long-time shadow, Eddie Chester, approached the other end of the stage where they were completing <u>Me and My Shadow</u>, Edwards stepped out from behind the curtain and broke in before Ted Lewis could sing the song's last words, "*...all alone and feeling blue.*"

"Excuse me, Ted. Pardon me for interrupting your rehearsal.

My name is Ralph Edwards. Right now we're on television, coast-to-coast, as I say to you, famous as the King of Jazz, Pied Piper of Happiness, the High Hatted Tragedian of Song, Ted Lewis, This is Your Life."

It was a subdued and restrained Ted Lewis who looked at Ralph Edwards, a stranger who was about to parade before the world this celebrated entertainer's life. "I'm flabbergasted," a serious, unsmiling Ted Lewis said. "I've never been so surprised in my life. I don't know what to say". He took out his handkerchief and turned his back to the audience. He looked as if he wiped tears from his eyes before he returned the handkerchief to his pocket and turned again towards the audience.

"Will you please accompany me to our This is Your Life studio," Edwards continued, "and go back with us through the years as a perennially popular showman whose battered hat, twirling opera stick, dancing hands, syncopated clarinet have made you a show business legend?"

Back at This is Your Life studio, Edwards led Ted Lewis on stage to the strains of the entertainer's theme song, When My Baby Smiles at Me. When the television host asked the audience, "Is everybody happy?" everyone went wild, clapping and shouting as he escorted an obviously stunned Ted Lewis to a seat on a park bench with a full screen photo of Ted Lewis Park in Circleville, Ohio, as a backdrop.

"You're very proud of your hometown," Edwards said, "and you always mention it during your performances. Let's imagine we're in the park in Circleville named in your honor, the Ted Lewis Park, right?"

Now, completely somber, Ted Lewis barely nodded.

"June sixth, eighteen hundred and ninety, is an especially happy day for the Friedman family. A second son, Theodore Leopold Friedman, is born to Pauline and Benjamin Friedman. That's you, Ted."

Ted Lewis was obviously uncomfortable in this

unfamiliar stage role of guest instead of entertainer. He continued to be subdued, quite, and inanimate, as I watched a Ted Lewis who was a complete stranger to the audiences, and to me, who were accustomed to his exuberant and magical stage presence. This Ted Lewis bore no similarity, except for the high hat that he still wore, to the enchanting celebrity Edwards had just introduced. He seemed to be buried in his own, far away thoughts.

Well, Teddy, you might as well sit back and enjoy this. There's no place to run to. Like it or not, the whole world is now going to know what your private life is all about.

Me and My Father's Shadow

Book Two

Ted

Chapter Twenty-Three

"Egyptian-Ella"

Theodore Leopold Friedman was nine years old and hated sweeping out his father's store. There was, in fact, nothing about working in Friedman's Bazaar that he liked. *Even if the ladies who shopped here did let me wait on them, I wouldn't like it.* In 1899, the proper Ohio women of Circleville in particular, and of Pickaway County in general, were horrified at the very idea of buying corsets, panties, or stockings from a male clerk. Proper ladies who shopped at Friedman's Bazaar would allow themselves to be waited on only by other women. Because Theodore and his four brothers, Edgar, Milton, Leon, and Max did not fit that category, from the time that each of the five boys was old enough to work in his parents' dry goods store, he was restricted to manual labor and deliveries. Being a clerk was out of the question.

Theodore's thoughts were far removed from the growing mound of debris forming in front of him as he pushed dirt and trash along the floor with a broom that was too long for his short stature and slight frame. His mind harbored more important things till he thought it would burst. Ever since he heard the most incredible news ever to hit Circleville, he could think of nothing else. An old German, Oscar Hammeringer, was in town to organize thirty boys into the Circleville Cadet Boys Band.

Now, more than anything else in the world, Theodore wanted to join. He just had to march with Oscar Hammeringer's band. But, I can't play an instrument, he thought. If I'm going to march in Mr. Hammeringer's band, I have to get something to play... and take music lessons. His dream, he decided, was to play the clarinet.

"No," Benjamin Friedman said in answer to his son's pleas to join the band, "and that is that. I'll not hear of it, Theodore. Not you. Not your brothers. How do you think it makes your mother and me look if our customers...or, even worse, the rest of the town, for that matter... see the Friedman boys march around town blowing screeching horns, or... beating senseless drums. Foolishness. All foolishness."

Theodore knew better than to argue with his father who worshiped the God of Hard Work, a generous Deity who bestowed well-earned rewards upon the self-made man. For his sons, Benjamin Friedman could ask no less, and prayed each day that his sons follow in their father's frugal footsteps.

How many times had his father told him his own success story, similar to hundreds of other Jewish immigrants from Europe, whose Promised Land was New York, Boston, and eventually even as far west as Circleville?

"Ah, Teddy, my son," Benjamin said, calling Theodore by this seldom used name of endearment, now captured in a brief moment of reverie. "Every morning, I got up before dawn when it was still dark in Chillicothe, and hitched old Joseph up to my Huckster wagon. Then we'd go through town selling my notions door-to-door." Here Benjamin would stop his story. "Theodore," he asked, "did I ever tell you that Chillicothe was the first capitol in Ohio?" Theodore was always ready to say "yes," but Benjamin never waited for an answer. "Now, Theodore, comes the most important part. I saved my money. Always remember...save, save, save. I watched it grow until I had enough to...well, do you know what your mother and I did? We had enough to open Friedman's

Bazaar, right here in Circleville. Then, we watched the store grow, month-by-month, year-by-year. Look at us now. Aren't we the most successful dry goods department store in Pickaway County?" At this point his father would stand up, put his hands on Theodore's shoulders, look him in the eye and say, "Someday, Theodore, all of this will belong to you boys, when your mother and I are old and you take over our business. No father and mother could ever wish more for their children."

I love Mama and Papa. How can I tell him I don't want to work in his store? I want to play the clarinet and march down Main Street with Mr. Hammeringer's new band.

How or why Benjamin Friedman finally succumbed to his son's passion was perhaps the mystery of the younger Friedman's life. Did his mother convince Benjamin to let him join? Certainly the elder Friedman would never change his mind of his own accord. Nevertheless, not only was Theodore finally allowed to purchase a clarinet, but also once a week he could take private lessons from Mr. Hammeringer. "But you must earn your own money to buy this...this clarinet, as well as pay the twenty-five cents for your music lesson. Working for what you get makes you appreciate it, Theodore, and builds character. No son of mine will have such things given to him."

Theodore prayed silently that his father would not pat him on his head after this lecture on thrift, as he usually did when teaching him a life-lesson. His prayer, however, was ignored, and Theodore had to endure from Benjamin Friedman a cross between a tap and a massage on his young, dark head. He felt lucky this time. Somehow, his father left out his advice against sloth.

Theodore knew working for his clarinet and lessons meant additional hours working at Friedman's Bazaar, plus mowing lawns and working wherever else he could earn money. Nothing, he knew, was too much for his father to ask of him, just so he could learn to play the clarinet and march in the band.

When Benjamin Friedman agreed that his son, Edgar, could join his brother in the band, Theodore could not believe his good luck. Now the two oldest Friedman boys would be marching down Main Street together, passing right in front of his parent's store. How proud his mother and father would be to see Edgar with a cornet joined by Theodore playing his beloved clarinet.

"Sorry, son," a music store clerk told young Theodore after he had earned enough money to buy a beautiful black clarinet that he now held in his hands, "you can't play this. Your fingers are too small to reach the keys."

The clerk was right. No matter how hard he tried to stretch his hand over the silver keys mounted in the front of the clarinet, his nine-year-old fingers just would not reach. Theodore was devastated. Without a clarinet, how was he going to march in Mr. Hammeringer's band?

"Tell you what, young man," the clerk said as Theodore reluctantly gave him back the clarinet, "how about buying this?" He walked over to another shelf in the store and picked up a small instrument, then handed it to Theodore. "Start out with this," the clerk said. " It's called a piccolo and is much smaller than this clarinet." The clerk handed the piccolo to Theodore who examined each part before carefully placing each of his fingers where it belonged.

"See, Theodore? Your fingers fit." The clerk was as pleased as Theodore that his hand was big enough for the piccolo. "Now, don't get discouraged when you're learning. It's a little harder to play than the clarinet. But, after you practice and learn to play it, well then, come on back in a couple of years. Your hands will be bigger and I'll sell you your clarinet."

When Theodore returned to the same music store clerk two years later, he had mastered the piccolo and was anxious to purchase his beloved clarinet. "See how big my hands are?" he said to the clerk as he spread wide all ten fingers as far as he could.

"Theodore, your fingers are still to small to reach the keys on a full size clarinet. They have to grow longer."

"But, look," Theodore said as he stretched his fingers with all his might. "Won't they fit? Please let me try,"

It was useless. Even though his fingers had grown, they were still too short to reach each note properly. He sighed, and thought that he would just have to keep playing the piccolo *for the rest of my life.*

The clerk felt sorry for the young musician. "Theodore," he said, "I've been thinking. Have you ever heard of an E Flat clarinet?"

"No Sir," he said, "what's that, Sir?"

"Well, it's a little smaller than a regular size clarinet and has a very shrill sound. Usually it's only played in brass bands. You know, I think your fingers just might fit. Shall I order one and see if it works?"

A few weeks later, Theodore Friedman walked out of the same music store with the most beautiful E Flat clarinet anyone could possibly have. His fingers could reach the keys perfectly, and he loved its clear, high-pitched sound.

As he played in Circleville's hometown events during the next few years, Theodore and his clarinet were inseparable, especially in talent shows where he was always the hit of the show. In 1903 he played in Circleville's First Annual Pumpkin Show, and was thirteen, incurably obsessed with playing his clarinet in every event that came to town.

It could have been Phineas Taylor Barnum's "Greatest show On Earth" that fascinated Theodore the first day he saw a circus come to Circleville. This master showman's famous <u>Ringling Brothers Barnum and Bailey Circus</u> had survived beyond P.T. Barnum's death in 1893, and continued to thrill millions of children and adults as it toured the country, and Circleville was a favorite stop for most circuses. Like other young men who loved the "Big Top," Theodore was always one of Circleville's young men who endured long waits at the train depot, each hoping to be first choice to work with the circus when it arrived.

Theodore helped unload everything. But, animals were the best of all. How he loved marching in a parade with elephants, lions, tigers, and horses as they were led—the dangerous ones in cages— through Circleville streets. "I'm part of the circus and these animals are mine," he thought, at least for the short time the circus was in town.

When Uncle Tom's Cabin, a Minstrel Show play based on Harriet Beeches Stowe's famous anti-slavery book, hit Circleville, as with the circus, Theodore was there to help, and the players gave him a job. They put him in charge of leading several Bloodhounds in their parade that would pass down Main Street, advertising to citizens that the show was in town. Immediately he fell in love with these Minstrel shows as much as he loved the circus. *Mama and Papa are going to be so proud of me when they see me leading all these beautiful dogs right in front of their store.*

Theodore was wrong. "You embarrassed the whole family," his father told him that night. "How do you think your mother and I felt to have the whole town see you do such a foolish stunt...and our employees watching, too?"

Theodore told his father that he would not do it again, a promise he knew he could never keep. He had to find a way to march with the Minstrels and carry their banner the next time they came to Circleville. *Just like I have to march with the circus when it comes to town.*

Dr. Cooper's Medicine Show arrived in town on the tail of the departing Uncle Tom's Cabin, fully equipped with his patent medicine, an elixir promising cures for every plague known to mankind. The objects of some of these maladies were displayed in little bottles filled with alcohol. Each of his favorites wore a label denoting its content:

> 1. Tapeworms: Three in a bottle filled with alcohol.
> 2. Appendix: One in a bottle filled with alcohol.

Today, Circleville's upstanding and honorable citizens of America's heartland would be healed of ailments they never knew they had. It would all be done with Dr. Cooper's miracle potion-in-a-bottle at the unheard of low cost of fifty cents, a paltry sum for eternal health.

When Dr. Cooper let it be known that he needed someone in town to announce his Medicine Show, he was thrilled when a teenage boy applied for the job. At first he was not sure why, but this young man seemed different from other boys who wanted the job. The Doctor employed him based on his own instinct.

Theodore Leopold Friedman was so elated when Dr. Cooper hired him, he would gladly have worked for nothing. Dr. Cooper was more than pleased with Theodore who was equipped with a rather strange looking clarinet. "It's an E Flat," Theodore explained. When Dr. Cooper heard how well Theodore played his clarinet, he knew that its captivating sounds played by this young artist would surely draw a crowd.

The medicine man was right. Theodore was like the Pied Piper of Hamelin as people started to gather around his new employee. Then, as the crowd grew larger, Theodore decided to expand his role and add some jokes.

"Why did the chicken cross the road?" he asked the crowd in front of him. No one answered. "Why, my good friends, to get to the other side, of course." His audience laughed. "But, do you know the real reason why a fireman wears red suspenders?" Again, silence. "Let me share this secret with each of you." Theodore leaned towards the audience as if to share a well-guarded confidence. "A fireman wears red suspenders...to keep his pants up." This time the audience roared so loudly their laughter could be heard almost throughout much of Circleville.. They loved him and his act. Mesmerized by his music, his wit, the crowd followed him down the street, marching to his music's beat.

A parade was forming behind Theodore and Dr.

Cooper, the Medicine Man now holding the reins as he guided his horse through Circleville streets, sitting high and proud on the seat of his Hansom cab. Red flares that led to a corner where the show would be held lined the edge of the street as the horse clopped along its path. Doctor Cooper wore a silk high hat and a swallowtail coat with five-dollar gold pieces for buttons. Its cuffs were held together by two and one-half dollar gold pieces used for studs. Two large ten dollar gold pieces decorated the back of his coat, and he threw out change to make sure the crowd followed him to his final destination, a corner where the show would begin. He smiled to himself, knowing that he would leave town tonight, not only with a good portion of Circleville's money, but also with the best E Flat clarinet player in Pickaway County. He knew that, from this day on, Theodore had to be part of his show.

"I do want to go with you, Sir," Theodore said when Dr. Cooper offered to include Theodore in his show permanently, "but, I'll have to ask my father first." *He'll never let me go.*

"Don't worry, son. You can let him know where you are later...when we get to our next stop."

"But, I heard you tell all those people who bought medicine today that you'd be here for three or four days. You said they could bring it back if it didn't work. Remember?"

"Oh, that. Change of plans, Theodore. Have to leave tonight. Are you coming?"

The new star of Dr. Cooper's Medicine Show hesitated, then said, "I guess I could wait till tomorrow to tell my father. Okay, Sir, let's go."

"Why did you run away from home again?" said Benjamin Friedman after he brought Theodore back to Circleville. This was the third time Theodore had "run off" to be with Dr. Cooper and the third time his father went to get him and bring him back home where he gave his son longer work hours at the store as punishment.

"I didn't run away, Papa. I was coming back." *How can I tell him I hate sweeping out the store and I hate delivering packages after school. There's never any fun here. Papa won't understand how much I love playing the clarinet and telling jokes in Dr. Cooper's show.*

When Theodore played clarinet for the Hoochie-Koochie dancers at the new carnival in town, as each girl removed one of her seven colorful transparent gauze shawls during their <u>Dance of the Seven Veils</u>, such impropriety proved too much for his father. Once again he dragged his son home and reprimanded him for his behavior.

"I don't know what to do with him anymore," he told Pauline Friedman. "I'm sorry I ever let Edgar and Theodore join that band."

"Papa," Theodore answered, when confronted by his father to explain why he kept disobeying him, "I guess I don't know. Except...I just have to be part of these shows and carnivals. Papa, please understand. It's just that...well...that show business is in my blood." He wanted to add, "It's as simple as that, Papa." But he didn't. He knew Papa did not think it was simple at all.

The barbers at Cricket's Barbershop in Circleville cut men's hair and played jazz, a musical beat unfamiliar to most Americans and Theodore at the beginning of the twentieth century. While Benjamin Friedman may have forced Theodore to keep his hair trimmed at Cricket's, his son was a willing disciple of the new sound and spent most of his free time in the shop, listening to the barbers play their jazz notes on a banjo and mandolin.

"Can I play my clarinet with you?" Familiar words to these new-jazz musicians who welcomed the young man and his horn into their group. The sound of Theodore's clarinet was perfect for their jazz. Their jazz was perfect for Theodore's clarinet. He was ready to expand his talent.

Wild Rosie was hyped in carnival posters placed around town, as the most ferocious, man-eating wild man in carnival history. This most recent show to set up in Circleville had hired

Theodore to spiel for the exhibit and play his horn to attract the crowds. First night Carnival goers, drawn by shrill, high-pitched notes and a strange new staccato beat blown from this dark-haired, slightly built young man with a horn, now were gathered in front of a small outdoor stage. Most of those watching had never heard of "jazz" that the young man was playing on his clarinet, but they listened, awestruck. Suddenly, he stopped playing, dropped the clarinet to his side, and began his spiel.

"He neither walks, nor talks, but he makes his wants known by grunts, growls, and groans," ballyhood Theodore. Then he put the horn to his lips and continued playing the same jazz music from his small clarinet. Circleville's ladies, farmers, and gentlemen were convinced by his music and spiel that they had to see the show. When Theodore finished, they rushed towards the young musician to buy tickets for one dime. Each was so intrigued by what Theodore had said, and his music, everyone just had to go inside and see this horrible monster.

Wild Rosie was a hit. As the crowd emerged from the show, everyone was somber, and scared to death at the horrible sight they just witnessed. There he was, Wild Rosie snarling, his swollen lips dripping with human blood from cadavers now reduced to raw bones surrounding Wild Rosie, forever confined in a deep, dimly lit pit. As each person passed by him, Wild Rosie growled ferociously as if to eat anyone of them, should someone be unlucky enough to fall into the pit and into the hairy arms of this crazed man-eater, his mouth now framed by blood-stained remains of recent victims.

Once outside and overcome with terror, everyone who saw Wild Rosie could talk of nothing else except the grisly sight inside. Outside, the crowd waiting to get in to see the next show, listened to every word they said, and could hardly wait to get in to see this savage human beast for themselves, hoping they would also come out alive. One dime was small price to pay for eternal horror.

The spectators had been fooled. Wild Rosie was actually a young man from Circleville named Schlistler, whose body was painted like a monster with a wig placed on his head. Then he was put into the pit with raw beef bones strewn all around him as if he had just eaten alive all of the previous spectators.

"Never again," said Benjamin Friedman as he brought Theodore back home one more time, giving him extra work time at Friedman's Bazaar. "This is the last time, or else," he threatened. The "or else" turned out to be removing Theodore from Everett High School and enrolling him at Bliss College business classes in Columbus, twenty-five miles from Circleville. With this education, his son would have a profession that would bring pride to the entire Friedman family. Perhaps he would even take over running Friedman's Bazaar someday.

Theodore, in the meantime, had become an accomplished whistler. In Columbus he discovered an outdoor band that gave concerts in the park and began whistling along with the music. This was certainly a lot more fun than learning business skills at Bliss.

One day his father needed something for his store from Columbus, and wanted Theodore to pick it up and bring it home with him that evening. He called up the college and asked to speak to his son.

"Why, Mr. Friedman," the head of the college said as he answered his ringing phone. "This is a surprise. How may I help you?

He paused and listened to Mr. Friedman.

"But, Mr. Friedman, Sir, I don't understand. Otherwise I would be happy to ask Theodore to pick up the new shirts for you."

He paused again as Mr. Friedman continued to speak on the other end of the line.

"I'm sorry, Sir, I would gladly tell Theodore to pick them up if I could. But, Sir, we have a very big problem here. I can't tell him that. I can't tell him anything. He isn't in school today for me to tell him anything. In fact, Mr. Friedman, your son hasn't been attending classes for the past two weeks."

"Hello, Papa," Theodore said as he got home that night.

"Hello, Theodore, how are you getting along at school," Benjamin said.

"Just fine, Papa."

"Come back in the office, please. I want to talk to you," said Benjamin Friedman who finally determined that, in Theodore's case, to spare the rod had already spoiled his second son. Theodore got whipped and more time added to sweeping out the store, along with his Uncle Simon, as punishment.

This time Benjamin admitted defeat and knew this probably was Theodore's last time at school. He could not, however, give up on his son entirely. He would make one more try. Already he was planning what to do about Theodore's next escape from Circleville. He had to establish a normal and acceptable career for his errant boy.

Chapter Twenty-Four

"Headin' For Better Times"

The man lay motionless on the bed, covered only by a white sheet. His eyes were closed, head wet with perspiration, now sunken into a pillow encased by an alabaster white pillowcase, a backdrop of contrast to his thick, tangled, dark brown hair, gray-accented at the temples. He was suffering, and had the look of both youth and old age, as if his weakened body could not decide whether to live or die.

A young girl, too thin for her fifteen years, seemed lost in the oversize wooden rocking chair she pulled so close to his bed that its rockers touched its low mattress as she rocked. On the bed, her elbows rested next to his body, her hands folded as if in prayer, and head propped upon her entwined fingers. As her lips moved, no sound came, although if one tried to read her lips, he might think she was saying, "Daddy, Daddy. Please don't die." Indeed, that was the case, confirmed by an identical subtitle that repeated her voiceless request, those same words written at the bottom of a movie screen where this drama was being performed.

Circleville's Exhibit Theater near Court Street at 122 West Main, was one of the first movie houses in the country to show the new 1911 silent film hit, The Lonedale Operator, starring Blanche Sweet, Francis J. Grandon, and Wilfred Lucas, and was playing to a packed house. For seventeen minutes - sixteen

frames per second for those in the audience who counted such
modern-day photographic miracles - Circleville's movie-goers
sat mesmerized by this visual drama unfolding before them.
Directed by D.W. Griffith and written by Mack Sennett, the saga
told the story of how this young girl took over her father's job as a
telegraph operator in a remote western town after he becomes ill.
She receives a message announcing a train's arrival that is carrying payroll money for a nearby mining company. Also on board
are two gangsters who plan to steal the money when it arrives at
the station. When it does, the gangsters accost the girl. While
captive, she is able secretly to wire for help then holds off the
badmen until lawmen arrive. The young girl saves the day, her
father recovers, and the good guys live happily ever after, a "must"
to satisfy any turn-of-the-century silent film audience.

After "The End" splashed across a black screen in bold,
white letters, the audience clapped, remained seated, and awaited
the next feature film, a rerun of The Great Train Robbery, Hollywood's first Western movie genre in 1903. A short stage show
between the two films would entertain these moviegoers while a
projectionist could rewind, by hand, The Lonedale Operator.

Once again theater lights went out. Only the stage was lit.
From one corner came music from an old upright piano, the
young pianist seated at a round, turntable piano seat. He had
just provided background music for The Lonedale Operator,
with piano improvisations apropos to each scene as it appeared
in the movie. Sometimes he played at a fast tempo with loud,
crashing effects to depict scenes of horsemen trying to out run a
racing train. Others were gentle episodes of soft, heart-rending
tones as the young girl prayed for her dying father. Now, during
intermission, he played several popular song favorites, When Irish
Eyes Are Smiling, Moonlight Bay, and You Made Me Love You,
before he ended with Peg o' My Heart. After he finished, everyone
applauded while few added polite, subdued cheers. As the pianist
began an introduction to My Meloncholy Baby, a hush filled the

theater and all eyes turned toward the stage as they heard....

"*Come to me my Melancholy Baby*," a voice from off stage half sang, half talked the song which grew louder with the words, "*Cuddle up and don't be blue.*" Half way through "*All your fears and foolish fancies may be,*" the vocalist appeared on stage in full view, walked slowly toward center stage where he stopped, faced the audience, then ended with "*Smile my honey dear, While I kiss away each tear, Or else I shall be melancholy, too.*" As he finished, he raised the black clarinet in his hand to his lips and started to blow into the horn. Accompanied by Oscar Y. Young, the Exhibit's new pianist, Theodore Friedman played two more choruses of <u>Melancholy Baby</u> on his clarinet. So moved was tonight's audience by Theodore and Oscar's duet, the crowd made them perform three more songs before they would let them stop and allow <u>The Great Train Robbery</u> to begin.

Benjamin Friedman, who deemed movie houses as distasteful as carnivals, circuses, and minstrel shows, was angry when he discovered Theodore was performing at The Exhibit.

"Without telling me?" he said to Theodore when he confronted him with this outrage. "Please leave that place... immediately," he said, and walked out of his study, leaving the Prodigal Son to repent of his most recent wayward sin.

For the first time, Theodore obeyed without argument, and Benjamin gloried in victory.

"Pauline," he told his wife, "I want to do something for Teddy. Let him know I only want what's best for him. What do you think about taking him and his friend, Oscar, with us to New York? We have another buying trip coming up next month and Oscar seems like a nice boy." *Finally Theodore is interested in my business.*

"Oh, Papa, how grand. I'll write to Ma Cook and make reservations. Teddy and Oscar will be so pleased." She smiled, kissed her husband on his cheek, and went to the study for writing paper, pen and ink. She knew reservations must be confirmed immediately before Benjamin changed his mind.

The first thing Theodore did when he, his parents and Oscar arrived at Ma Cook's, was to show Oscar Ma Cook's picture gallery that almost covered her walls and furniture. A few of these photographs were of entertainers, his favorites, who had at one time stayed at Ma Cook's. Each of these particular photos was as familiar to Theodore as an old friend, and he delighted in telling Oscar who each one was as he took the pianist on tour through Ma Cook's boarding house.

"That's John McCormack," Theodore said, "And that up there is Ellen Beach Yaw, you know, the opera star they call <u>Lark Ellen</u>? And over here is Marie Dressler next to Maude Adams." Theodore was almost reverent in front of a picture of a muscular man in shackles, nude except for an under shorts type of costume. "Here's Houdini," he told Oscar, touching the black frame as he spoke. "See Lillian Gish and her sister, Dorothy, next to Harry Carey... over there?" He pointed to the opposite wall in the dining room.

It was New York's Broadway, with its daytime hubbub and chaos in contrast to a nighttime overflowing with sparkle and glitter from thousands of glowing lights that danced and blinked while moving in haphazard random, that drew Theodore like a moth to a flame to this famous Great White Way. He could hardly wait to show it to Oscar. *He's going to get as excited as I do when he sees it tonight.* The tour, however, would have to wait until tomorrow.

"Ma Cook wants us all, including you, Oscar, to visit with her and some of her guests after dinner tonight. You'll have to wait until tomorrow to see the city," Benjamin told the two young men.

At 7 a.m. sharp the next day, breakfast was served after those staying with Ma Cook gathered together at a long, picnic length table in Ma's simple, but tastefully decorated dining room. Usually this was a favorite part of those seldom times Theodore accompanied his parents on their buying trips to New York. At Ma Cook's breakfast table Theodore loved hearing about the other guests' world of excitement, so far removed from Circleville's mundane realities, as they came together and shared stories about their lives. Today, however, he was anxious to show Oscar New York's Great White Way. Politely, they excused themselves early from the group, and left to launch their day's adventure.

"We'll be late, so don't wait up for us," Theodore called back to his parents as he opened the front door. The boys ran down the front steps to the sidewalk, where he and Oscar began their half-hour trek to Columbus Circle and Central Park West, where they began their discovery of Broadway's Great White Way.

Before Oscar and Theodore had returned to Ma Cook's Boarding House late that night, their zigzag path had taken them in a haphazard course along most streets on The Great White Way. It was given an arena on Broadway far too small to accommodate properly its overflow of theaters and restaurants that were now squeezed together too tightly onto an inadequate twelve block square piece of New York soil. Sometimes they walked along Broadway. Other times they went in and out of, or up and down, its famous side streets, such as Thirty-ninth Street, Forty-second Street, Seventh Avenue, Forty-fifth Street, or Thirty-second Street. More often the two young musicians doubled back on themselves as they tried to walk every inch of this city's incomparable tribute to theater, making sure not to miss some important place.

Beginning at Thirteenth Street, "The Way" traced its mile-and-a-half passageway along the Avenue to Forty-fifth Street, and many New Yorkers were still undecided as to which part was the beginning or the end. It was during this trek that Oscar and Theodore passed Ziegfeld's <u>New Amsterdam Theater</u> with its <u>Midnight Frolics</u>, and George M. Cohan's new theater presenting for the first time Cohan's new musical, <u>Little Johnny Jones,</u> at Broadway and Forty-third Street. Farther on they passed by <u>The</u>

Belasco featuring <u>The Girl in Waiting</u> and staring Laurette Taylor, <u>The Republic</u>, The Music Hall at Twenty-ninth Street, Vaudeville theaters advertising their specialty acts, and bawdy Burlesque houses taunting each male passersby with promises of temptation within.

"It's just like you described, Teddy," Oscar had said as they had watched evening shadows darken the city's bright daylight. With a sudden explosion of brilliance pouring from thousands of electric lights, The Great White Way turned into a land of magical white glory. "As if every star in heaven fell on Broadway," said Oscar who thought for a minute, turned to Theodore, then asked, "Is that why they call it 'The Great White Way?'"

"That's right," Theodore had said, and both of them stood silent, mesmerized by the dancing bright glow of illuminated letters that spelled out messages to both pedestrians and motorists below as the words moved across this sign high above Times Square.

Once back in Circleville, Oscar returned to the Exhibit Theater and his piano. Theodore, however, was convinced more than ever that he had to return to Broadway and pursue his own dream of a career in show business.

"Papa, I have to go back," he said, wishing that Benjamin would understand why he had to leave both Circleville and his father's own dream for him to work in Friedman's Bazaar. He knew, instead, that it would break his father's heart knowing his second son would never work in his business again. It was a silence of death from his father, followed by tears that ran down Papa's face that Theodore was not he prepared for, as the old man turned away from his boy and walked out of the room.

Benjamin's loss was Gus Sun's gain. When the small-time vaudeville promoter hired Theodore and his brother Edgar to perform on his Gus Sun Circuit, Benjamin was devastated.

"Now I am loosing two sons?" Benjamin had said after the boys had told their father they were going to do a slapstick comedy together in vaudeville, and had already been hired by Gus Sun after they auditioned for him. Their father was too stunned to say more, except to give the boys his blessing, and reminded them that he and the store were waiting for them when they failed in this new endeavor, which he was sure would be within a month after they started.

Convincing Edgar to join him in a two-man act had not been easy.

"Look, Ed," Theodore had said, "I want you to hear this recording before you decide. It's about Ethnic Humor...you know, where races make fun of themselves and other races... and two Jewish comics do this routine about an old German named Meyer trying to put one over on a dumb Dutch immigrant named Mike. Weber plays Meyer, and Fields plays Mike. It's called, 'I'm a Gizzard,' done by Weber and Fields" said Theodore as he read the disc label. Then he placed it on an old Victrola standing against a wall in their parent's home, wound it, and placed the arm that held a needle on to the record. The two young men sat down to listen.

I'm a Gizzard

"The Hypnotist"
(Music plays)
Lew Fields: Ha, ha. How are ya, Mike?
Joe Weber: Hello, Meyer
Fields: Say, Mike.
Weber: What?
Fields: Did I tell ya whet I was?
Weber: What is it?
Fields: I'm a mesmerist.
Weber: A what?
Fields: A mesmerist.
Weber: What is that?
Fields: You know...a gizzard (wizard).
Weber: A gizzard?

Fields: Yes. I can, I can, I can look at you, and you close your
    eyes, and make you do as you don't want to do.

Weber: Oh, you mean a tipmohist (hypnotist).

Fields: a tipmohist (hypnotist),that's the idea. Yes.

Weber: Ah, I see.

Fields: Did you ever have that done?

Weber: No, I never was.

Fields: I can do it.

Weber: Let's try on it.

Fields: Sure, sure. Look at me. Now, close your eyes. Now open
    your mouth. Now close your eyes. Open your mouth.
    Close your eyes!

Weber: Oh, no, no. I had that already.

Fields: What?

Weber: I know that game. Shut your eyes and open your
    mouth.

Fields: No, no. That ain't a game. Here, look at me. Now, close
    your eyes. Stand still...You feel something?

Weber: You got a hose in your mouth.

Fields: No, gracious, no. Look for the light.

Weber: Who does?

Fields: Does what?

Weber: With his wife?

Fields: Gracious. Now here, stand here. Now look at me. Now
    close your eyes. Now, Mike, you think the same as I'm
    thinking.

Weber: If I do that, we're fired.

Fields: Gracious. Will you listen to me, please? How can I get
    power over you, you don't stand and listen?

Meyer: You can have me.

Fields: I don't want you. Now, when you open your eyes, you'll
    imagine you're traveling in the Twentieth Century train.
    The train is going very fast, so hold on to the strap. Open
    your eyes. Brrrrp! You're off. You're in Chicago! You're in

Cincinnati! You're in Pittsburgh! You're in Baltimore! You're in Washington! You're in Philadelphia! You're in Patterson! You're in New York! You're in New York! You're in New York! Mike! Mike! Come out of Patterson! Mike! Mike! Mike, please listen to me! I can't get him out of Paterson. Mike! Mike! He must have a girl in Patterson. All right, all right, all right.

Meyer: Ahhhh.

Fields: Ha, ha. I'm glad you come to. Well, what do you think of it?

Meyer: I fooled ya: I was in Brooklyn all the time!

Both men laughed when it was over.

"It's even funnier when you see them on the stage, Ed," said Theodore. "Fields is tall and Weber is short, and both have beards and wear derbies with the craziest loud checks on them you ever saw."

"I don't know, Teddy. If I leave the University and the store, what'll it do to Papa?"

"Look, Ed, I've got this idea for a comedy slapstick in black face. Remember what a success Bert Williams is? He's at the top just by making good-natured fun of his own race. Well, I think we can do it, too. Only, my idea is for us to be more like Weber and Fields...two working together. I've even got a name for the act. The Warden and the Coon. We'll have a dialogue, sort of like Weber and Fields, and bring our instruments into it, too. Some songs, maybe? Oh, come on, Edgar, this would be a great start for us in show business."

Gus Sun thought so, too. The minute the "small time show" promoter and head of the Gus Sun Circuit, saw them audition the act, he knew he had a winner. Gus may have represented only tabloids, or "tab" shows as they were called, low budget, miniature vaudeville shows and musical comedies that played in the small towns around rural America, but he knew talent when he saw it, "...especially that Theodore..." and he knew how to market it. *Their act is just what every inexpensive movie house in North America is looking for. So it isn't the "Big Time." There's plenty of money in "tabs," and I'm just the guy to do it right.*

"Welcome aboard, Gentlemen," Gus said after they signed their contract. Let's begin. We have a lot of work to do. But, first of all, let's give you a decent stage name. From now on, boys, you're "Ted and Ed."

That summer, Gus Sun booked them in cities like Springfield, Ohio, Cattleburg, Kentucky, Huntington, Virginia, Wheeling, West Virginia, and Barburton, Ohio. Ted and Ed made $22.50 a week. Out of that, they paid their own expenses, and room and board could be as much as $1.75 a day. "These hard times are worth it," thought Ted, now that he and Edgar were one of the ninety other types of vaudeville acts booked throughout Small Town, USA. Like other performers in these shows, Ted hoped one day to play the "Big Time," the goal of every miniature show entertainer.

Existence for Ted and Ed was rigorous as they performed six shows a day in miserable, musty theaters that were like furnaces in the summer and ice boxes in the winter. Ted, however, loved every uncomfortable minute of it, no matter how miserable they were. This was show business and his idea of heaven no matter what the conditions. In all the theaters where they were booked, they played to audiences who loved their act, and Ted and Ed were always a hit.

Ed increasingly dreamed of his comfortable life at home and at Ohio State University and disliked the cheerless, jarring, and pitiful pay on the Circuit. Memories of his life as it once was, remained a persistent reminder of the comfort his life had been back in Ohio, and an enticing alternative to this new life style should he decide to quit. But, he knew how much Ted loved show business, and could not abandon him now. For the time being, Edgar had to endure the exhausting pace. Besides, they were now in New York for a short time and were enjoying the comfort of Ma Cook's Boarding House. They would also use this as an opportunity to show the publishers on Tin Pan Alley what they could do on stage with their clarinet and cornet when they auditioned in one of the small, private booths reserved for hopeful performers on the Alley.

Throughout Tin Pan Alley, Popular songs poured out daily from hundreds of music publishers' windows. By the time this music hit the sidewalks of 48th Street it, sounded as if hundreds of kitchen pans bombarded the cement below, each song causing a different tinny noise as it landed. It came mostly from pianos played inside these publishers' offices above when songwriters, both composers and lyricists, marketed their wares on pianos that were not always played solo, but often accompanied by trumpets, vocalists, trios and quartets, and an occasional string instrument. It all depended upon who or what was being auditioned. By the time these tunes escaped through the countless open windows, and fused with street sounds from automobile engines, horse carts, young boys playing in the street, dogs barking, or venders screaming out their daily wares, neither the original music from above, or the inevitable noise from below was distinguishable.

"My God, Teddy," said Edgar, as if feigning possible damage to his ears by covering them with his hands, "how do they keep their hearing in this madhouse?"

"Probably don't," his brother said, and laughed. "That's why they call it 'Tin Pan Alley.'"

What was hell to Edgar's ears was heaven to Ted's. He loved every raucous sound in this part of Manhattan's show business district that stretched from West 28th Street between Broadway and 6th Avenue, and was appropriately dubbed Tin Pan Alley by Monroe Rosenfeld, a journalist-turned-song writer and lyricist.

Harry Von Tilzer Music Company was one of many publishing houses whose music poured from these open windows and Harry Von Tilzer himself had won a special spot in Tin Pan Alley history. Harry loved playing the piano, composing popular music, and he was usually found sitting at an old upright piano that he kept in his publishing firm. The piano's sound, however, was not to Harry's liking and did not please his musical ear. To adapt the piano to the sound he wanted, Harry experimented with various manipulations of his piano strings until he was satisfied with what he heard. The wonderful tinny sound he was looking for finally occurred one day after Harry stuffed paper between the strings of the piano's harp that was encased inside its body.

When Rosenfeld heard the harsh, metalic sound that Harry created, it suggested to him a title for a piece of music he was writing. Rosenfeld named the song, <u>Tin Pan Alley.</u> Eventually the title name would refer to the entire publishing area in Manhattan, and also had become the generic term for all publishers of popular music, regardless of geographic location. Tin Pan Ally was one of the musical wonders of the world.

Ted and Ed had auditioned for several publishers on the "Alley," and were now on their way to audition for Harry Von Tilzer.

"If he doesn't want us, Ed, I guess we call it quits," said Ted.

The minute Harry auditioned Ted and Ed, he knew he was seeing a champion act. Especially impressed by one of the young musicians, Tilzer was fascinated with the unusual way he played his clarinet, and the fascinating way he combined this music with his antics on stage, resulting in a unique humor to the act.

"Ted," Tilzer said when they were alone, "you've got a captivating charisma and audiences are going to love you. Don't get big headed and lose it. Just be yourself and you're headed for the Big Time. I know exactly where you should start."

"William," Harry said as he called his friend, William Hammerstein, Theater Manager and Director of Hammerstein's Victoria Theater, "you've gotta come over and see this new act. Especially the clarinet player."

When William Hammerstein booked Ted and Ed for two

weeks at the Victoria, it meant that the Friedman brothers were now playing at one of the best theaters in the country. Finally, they were courting the Big Time.

It also meant that they were on the same bill as Will Rogers who was also playing at the Victoria. Roger's folksy humor that accompanied his roping skills learned while growing up on a large ranch in the Cherokee Nation, plus his captivating homespun banter, gained him celebrity in Vaudeville. "I never met a man I didn't like," he quipped as he twirled a lasso above his head, jumped through it, then added as he lowered the lasso and jumped in and out of it several times, "All I know is what I read in the newspapers." Ted and Will Rogers became great friends during the next two weeks he and Ed were at the Victoria.

Walker and Williams was another vaudeville comedy team that was on the same bill as Will Rogers, and Ted and Ed, and was one of the most renown and successful stage partnerships in American theater during a time when white actors in black face were popular with both races.

Williams and Walker pioneered this new kind of "black" humor, and had developed their own company, opening the door for other black actors, singers, dancers, and musicians, "...redefining the boundaries of legitimate Negro Theater."

Ted and Ed were now approaching Big Time, and were signed up by a small, little known agency named Wilburn and Vincent. Along with a new singer they added to their act, they toured and performed in towns like Youngstown and Akron, Ohio. Their success was short lived, however, when the singer fell in love and left the team, and Edgar told Ted, "I'm going to leave the act, too, and go home. I hope you understand, Teddy."

With his brother gone, Ted was now completely alone and lonely. *I miss Edgar.* He was again a single act, committed to show business, and returned to New York feeling as if he were starting over. *Well, I did it before. I can do it again.*

El Dorado Café was a sleazy cellar that specialized in dragging customers from off the street, then throwing them out when they got too drunk, and where an occasional waiter was either a murderer or dope addict.

"What's your line?" Herman Moss, the owner of El Dorado Café asked when Ted applied for a job.

"Well, Sir..."

"Hey, cut out the 'sir' stuff, will ya? I'm Moss. Herman Moss. Leave 'sir' for the upper crust."

"Certainly, Mr. Moss, uh, Herman. Is 'Mr. Moss' okay?"

"Sure, Sure," Herman Moss said as he laughed. Either is fine. Now, tell me, what do ya do.

"Well, I play the clarinet or saxaphone. Which ever you want ...or both." In a rare moment of resignation to his son's choice of profession, Benjamin had bought him a C Melody saxophone on one of his New York buying trips. Ted could now play it as well as his clarinet, but was his second choice as a favorite.

"Let's hear ya...on both."

Ted played a current popular number on each instrument, then put them down.

"What do you think, Mr. Moss?"

Herman Moss thought for what seemed an eternity to Ted, then said, "Your hired. Can't pay much, but we'll talk about that tomorrow. Let's see how ya handle the customers tonight. Can ya begin that soon?"

"You bet I can, Mr. Moss," said Ted, grinning at his good fortune. "Can I change here? I don't have a place to stay, yet."

"Sure, sure. In fact, go check out the place. Ya might be here a long time." *That sax's the best thing I've heard in a month of Sundays. The Kid's got talent. Real talent.* Think I'll introduce ya tonight as, 'Saxy.'"

"Ladies and gentlemen, straight from a national tour and the Victoria theater, here's Saxy."

In keeping with the new name Herman Moss gave him,

Ted, began his routine on the saxophone, and played some of
the jazz that he learned with the boys at Cricket's Barber Shop in
Circleville.

"Hey, Saxy," one of the customers called out, "how about
somethin' a little more romantic?"

Ted changed the next few numbers to several popular songs,
and walked by the customer several times while he played them.

"Now, that's more like it, Saxy," he said, during one of the
times Ted passed by his table, and threw a quarter into Ted's
saxophone, the coin clanking as it hit the inside of the horn.
From then on, Ted's act consisted mostly of customers requesting
songs and Ted catching coins as they threw them into his horn.

Ted had been a success at the El Dorado Café for several
weeks when he approached his boss.

"Mr. Moss," he said, "My folks are coming to New York on
one of their buying trips for their store, and are bringing an old
friend with them. Mrs. McCoy from Circleville. I'd sure like to do
something nice for them while they're here."

"Sure, sure, Saxy," Mr. Moss said. "Anything special in
mind?"

"Well, I'd like to give them a party, but I don't have much
money."

His boss thought a few moments. "Tell ya what I'm gonna
do. Just leave that party to me. I'll come up with somethin' real
nice. Won't cost much, either. Okay?"

"That's really great, Mr. Moss. I'll invite them for Saturday
night when they get to Ma Cook's on Friday."

"Perfect, Saxy." Herman Moss went whistling into his office,
winking at Ted as he closed his door.

El Dorado Café, usually somber as a tomb before it
opened in the evenings, this Saturday was alive with unprec-
edented activity as its several waiters and two cooks hustled at
their appointed tasks in preparation for the "party" that evening.
Ted had come early to watch them, and had never seen any of

them so happy, clowning around, no longer stern and morose. They took special care with a white linen tablecloth spread on the special table assigned to the Friedmans where his parents and Mrs. McCoy would have an uninterrupted view of the show. He admired how they knew just where to place each item, the champagne glasses, linen napkins, and flatware, on the correct side of the elegant, flowered china that had remained hidden for so many years in the basement recesses of the El Dorado. One waiter in particular seemed to know what he was doing, and appointed himself overseer of Ted's dinner project. The other waiters obeyed his commands without complaint.

"Like it, Saxy?" his bossed asked, as he entered his café. He had been watching Saxy's reaction to these dinner plans, and seemed delighted that his saxophone player was so pleased.

"Everything's wonderful, Mr. Moss." Then Ted pointed towards the special glasses set at each place. "But, I can't afford champagne."

"Don't worry, Saxy." Then Mr. Moss leaned over and whispered in his ear. "It ain't really champagne. It's celery tonic, and the guys are going to serve it in classy champagne bottles like it's the real stuff. Saxy, they'll never know the difference." He slapped Ted on the back and walked back to his office, laughing and shaking his head all the way.

Before he entered, he turned towards Ted and said, "Don't you have a worry in that dark, curly head of yours, Saxy, m'boy. Your folks got a great meal coming to 'em and I'm footin' the bill. Just keep blowin' that horn, Kid. That's all I ask." Herman Moss turned and disappeared into his office.

"Theodore, that meal was wonderful," Pauline Friedman said as her son took them back to Ma Cook's after their dinner at the El Dorado. "I'll drop that lovely Mr. Moss a 'thank you' note as soon as we get back. Wasn't it lovely, Benjamin?"

Her husband nodded, quietly answered "yes" to his wife, then added, making sure Theodore could hear, "Pauline, are you finished fixing up Theodore's room? Theodore, wait till you see what Mother has done to it. I know you'll love staying there."

Ted could not believe that his father still expected him to leave show business and come back to Circleville. He was speechless until he dropped off his parents at Ma Cook's and told them and Mrs. McCoy goodnight.

A few days after the Friedmans returned to Circleville, Herman Moss Called Ted into his office.

"Your dad was in here before he left," his boss said. "He told me everything was great and wanted to thank me. He and your mother loved your act and the champagne. Saxy, ya got one hell of a dad there."

"Yes, Mr. Moss, my father is a wonderful man."

"Glad to hear ya say that, Saxy. Seems to really look out for ya. Right?"

"All the time, Mr. Moss."

And wants what's best for ya. Right?"

"Absolutely."

"So, son, you're going to understand what I say next, then."

Well, yes, I...guess so?"

"Saxy, you're fired."

At first Ted could only stare at his employer. Finally, he said, "But, Mr. Moss, you really liked my act. What did I do wrong, Mr. Moss. Please, tell me."

"I love your act, and ya didn't do anything wrong. You're the best damn entertainer I've ever had. Herman Moss got up from his chair, came around to the front of his desk, and put his hand on Ted's shoulder.

"I don't want ya to leave, Ted. No one else who works here wants ya to, either. But, ya got to go. Your dad asked me to talk ya into going back home. I think he's right. Ya don't belong here, Ted. Ya come from class."

"I can't go back, Mr. Moss. Please try to understand. I love my parents. I love Circleville. But, I just have to be in show business. Don't fire me. I love it here. You can cut my salary if you want. I'll sweep the floor. I'll wash dishes. I'll do anything. Just... please, please let me stay."

"Saxy, I'm sorry. You've got to go home. Ya come from wonderful people who love ya, and this is no place for ya. Now, get your stuff together. Get out of here. Here's the money to get home." Herman Moss stuffed a hundred dollars in Ted's shirt pocket. "Go."

Chapter Twenty-Five

"Lonely Troubadour"

Gus Sun wanted Ted Friedman back as a client and was excited when he called.

"It's Ted, Gus. Can I come over and talk? I'm on my own, now...a single...and I'd sure like to have you represent me again." After the El Dorado and Herman Moss, Ted tried going back to Circleville, but returned to New York when the itch for show business took over.

"Well, I'll be damned. Ted. I was thinking about you. Come on over, buddy, and let's start you right away. I've got just the place for you."

In fact, during the next three months Gus had five bookings for him. Ted was fired from the first four of them.

"You've been fired again?" Gus screamed when Ted called the fifth time to tell him he lost his job. "Don't call any more, Ted. We're through."

Ted did try to call again, but each time Gus Sun refused his calls. When Ted decided to wire the promoter under assumed names...Jerry Walker, Murray Adams, or Dan Jones, to name a few attempts at an alias...it worked. Right away Ted received several more bookings from Gus.

"They just don't like my act," Ted told himself after each booking was cancelled after a few performances. Finally he decided, "I'm going home and really try to work at the store." When this latest "good intention" failed after a disagreement with his parents, Ted left again and took a job at Henry Goldsmith's Music Store in Columbus.

"You're going to be doing a little bit of everything around here, Ted. Clean instruments that I've collected. Sort of a hobby with me. The most important is demonstrating and selling these instruments displayed in my store. Seems, young man, that you play all of them pretty well, from what I've heard. And you'll sell records. Since we don't keep these stocked in the store, each time you sell a record you have to run down to the wholesale house and get a duplicate. Think you can do all that?"

"Yes, Mr. Goldsmith. I'm really looking forward to working here. And I want to thank you again for the opportunity." Ted smiled and shook his employer's hand.

Ted did like his new job, but dreams of New York with its Broadway, theaters on The Great White Way, and Tin Pan Alley took over. *That's where I want to be, no matter how much I like working here. I belong in show business.*

The first thing Ted Friedman did after quitting Mr. Goldsmith's Music store and arriving in New York City, he called his mother and told her where he was.

"I didn't want to worry you, Mama, and wanted you to know my good news. Mama, I've put a new act together with a great new partner. We've already got a booking down South. Yes, Mama, I promise to call more often."

Jack Lewis was the perfect partner for Ted Friedman. Not only was he a good character actor, but he was also an accomplished singer. When Ted first met Jack Lewis in New York and saw what Jack could do, he was sure that their combined talents would blend to form a great vaudeville team. After they worked up their act together, he was convinced that he made the right choice.

"'Lewis and Friedman' is going to be a sensation," Ted told

Jack.

Ted was right. With their new stage name of "Lewis and Friedman," plus a good act, they were doing great on the small time circuit, especially in the South, and their success made up for the meager wages they received. Show business was all that counted, and the two men looked eagerly towards their next booking in Greenville, North Carolina.

Both men were tired when they arrived in Greenville, but were anxious to get to their new job. They hurried to the tiny rooming house where they were scheduled to stay, dropped off their trunks without unpacking, and left to find the theater. They had arranged with the manager to rehearse and did not want to be late.

"It's supposed to be near here," Jack said as they reached the center of the tiny city.

"That must be the theater," said Ted, pointing to some blinking lights high above a sidewalk a few blocks away. "Let's go."

As an illuminated marquee came into view, Jack and Ted hurried faster so they could see their names in lights. As they approach the marquee and the letters on it became clear, both men stopped, were silent as they each read the words, "Lewis and Lewis," standing out like black onyx against the white light filled background.

"Ted, why have they got my name twice?"

"Beats me. You stay here, Jack, 'cause I'm sure going to find out."

Ted raced inside the theater through an open swinging door, then found another door inside with a bronze nameplate imprinted "Manager." He knocked once, threw open this door without waiting for an answer, and stormed into an office with a man sitting behind a large desk.

"What the hell..."

"Are you the manager?" said Ted Lewis, now glaring at

the man behind the desk who had jumped up and was coming around to the front of it.

"Yes, I'm the manager here. Just who do you think you are to come barging..."

"Well, I'm not Jack Lewis. He's out side and I'm his partner."

"Ted Friedman? My god, Ted, why'd you come busting in like that?"

"What's the idea of you just billing my partner?"

"What are you talking about, Ted?"

"'Lewis and Lewis' is what I'm talking about. Why isn't it 'Lewis and Friedman' up on the marquee...like the contract reads? Why did you bill my partner twice?"

The manager started to laugh, walked back to his chair, sat down.

"So, that's the problem. Ted, I didn't bill Jack twice. We just had a little problem with the marquee. That's all. Ted, sit down and let me explain."

Ted was still angry as he obeyed, and sat down on the edge of a chair in front of the manager's desk. "Okay. Go on. Explain."

"Ted," the manager began, "in case you didn't notice, this is a very small town, with a very small theater, and a very small marquee. 'Lewis and Friedman' just wouldn't fit. So, I decided to change the name to 'Lewis and Lewis.' Is it so bad that it will be Jack Lewis and Ted Lewis playing our theater while you're here?" Frankly, Ted, I think it sounds a hell of a lot better than 'Lewis and Friedman.'"

Ted began to relax, sat back in his chair, and after a few moments said, "No, I guess it doesn't matter. Okay, then 'Lewis and Lewis' it is.

Jack Lewis was leaning against the theater wall as Ted came out smiling. Ted walked up to his partner, grabbed his hand, and shook it as he said, "Jack, I'd like to introduce myself. My name is Ted Lewis."

After the Greenville booking, both Jack and Ted agreed that they needed an agent if they were going to make the Big Time.

"You boys are good," said "Happy" Harry Rapp, a New York agent who agreed to represent "Lewis and Lewis" as soon as he auditioned their act. "Keep your eye on that clarinet player," he told friends in the business. "Someday, everyone's going to know about 'Ted Lewis.'"

"Boys," said Happy, I've got you booked in Canada."

"Canada?" Ted and Jack said together.

"Happy," Ted said, "I thought we were going to Big Time?"

"You are, Ted, and this is a great place to start. It's a new vaudeville circuit up there. It'll give you about three months solid booking, then you can come back here and I'll have bookings in the big cities for you guys. Think of Canada as between Small Time and Big Time vaudeville. Okay?"

During November and December of 1913, and January of 1914, besides a reign of bitter cold, every little town and vaudeville house in Canada was miles and miles apart. Rooming houses had little or no heat and the theaters they played were freezing, musty, drafty, and reeked of foul mold and dirt. This was the "new vaudeville circuit" in Canada that Happy had promised, took them from Saskatuwan all the way up into Alberta, around Moose Jaw, and further north where conditions got worse. Even Ted, who cherished the worst circumstances in show business in the States, found Canada's wastelands almost impossible to endure.

Towards the end of these three months, things became intolerable when "Lewis and Lewis," were not paid and had to use their own savings to finance their trip.

"Ted," said Jack who was counting what little money remained, "we're broke."

Their tour had ended in Alberta and so had their money. Now stranded at Alberta's railroad depot and soaked by a freezing storm, they were forced to take refuge in the train station as they dashed inside to elude the savage weather.

"We have to have food," Ted said, and told Jack to wait inside the station while he went back outside to look around. Ted knew Jack was near exhaustion as his partner sat down, nodded "yes," and gave no objection to Ted's plan. Jack closed his eyes and immediately fell asleep, the back of his head resting on the top of a worn, wooden railway station seat.

"At least he won't know how miserable he is while I'm gone," thought Ted. The storm had subsided, and he walked outside into the black, icy night. *For the first time in my life, Theodore Leopold Friedman is going to have to beg for food.*

Ted had asked only a few people for help when he met a Chinese man that responded with a smile. Even though he seemed not to understand what Ted was saying, he must have guessed at his plight because he gave Ted a dime. Ted smiled back at him, then grabbed his hand and shook it as he said, "Thank you" over and over several times.

"Jack, wake up!" Ted shook his partner's shoulder gently.

"What? Oh, Ted, How'd it go?"

"Come on, Jack. Let's go eat." He held up the dime, which seemed to him like a fortune, for Jack to see. Both men were grinning as they went back out into the cold in search of an all night café. "Things aren't so bad, Jack. We have one entire dime and it's stopped raining."

As Jack and Ted sat at a small table reading the menu at a café they found just around the corner from the station, Jack said, "Ted, there's nothing on here we can buy with just a dime."

Ted got up from the table and walked up to the waitress behind the counter.

"Excuse me, Miss, may I speak to the owner."

"He's cleaning up and getting ready to close, but I'll ask." She walked into the kitchen through a swinging door.

In a few minutes, a slight, balding man came towards Ted while the waitress started to wipe down the tables and chairs.

"My friend and I have been touring this part of Canada," Ted said. "We're entertainers in vaudeville and are on our way home to New York. Sir, all we have left is one dime. Would it be possible to have something to eat for this ten cents?"

The man thought for a moment. "I can give you a bowl of beans. It's all I have left."

"Beans, sir, would be wonderful. We'll hurry and eat it so you can go home."

"No need. Take your time. I have work left to do before we close."

In a few moments the waitress brought over a large bowl of red beans with two spoons. She left, went into the kitchen, then came back. "The boss thought you might like this." She placed a half loaf of dark bread in front of them.

Jack and Ted looked at each other, then both men turned to the waitress. Jack said, "Please, tell your boss, 'thanks' for everything. This is the best meal we've ever had."

"Jack, I think we should get back to Winnepeg. We need to work and make some money." It was the next morning after their meal of beans and bread, and both Jack and Ted were feeling better after their meal and short rest in the railway station.

"Okay, Ted. But, how?" It takes three days on the Canadian Pacific to get to Winnepeg and we don't have any money."

"Stay here, Jack, and let me ask around."

When Ted saw a small group of train men joking and laughing, he walked up to them, introduced himself, and identified his profession before explaining his problem. Finally, Ted asked, "Do you know of any way we can get to Winnepeg?"

"Sure," one trainman said, "if you were only a Moose. All these trainmen belong to the Moose."

Ted laughed along with them and reached into his wallet. He pulled out a card and showed his membership card in the Moose brotherhood to the men. "I am a Moose. I joined in

Birmingham, Alabama. Here's my card."

"That's great," the trainman said. "This is what you do. There's an eight o'clock train in the morning. You take your trunk and see the man at the station and show him your card. Tell him your troubles and you'll get to Winnepeg. But, remember, it's a three-day trip."

Ted and Jack sat up all night in the station waiting for the train to come in. When it arrived, Ted found the conductor, showed him his Moose card, and told him his story.

The conductor took his card, looked at it and at Ted, then said, "I'm only going about a hundred miles from here where another conductor will take over. So, I'll tell him your story, you show him your card, and maybe he'll take you on farther. Don't forget that they change conductors several times during the trip. You do the same with each one."

From then on, the three-day trip to Winnepeg went on in relays as Ted explained his problem to each new conductor who promptly honored the Moose card.

"Where are we going to sleep, Ted?" The conductor who just came on duty took Jack and Ted to the Smoker car and told them to sit there. He was delighted that Ted was a fellow Moose, and made sure they were comfortable. "And, what are we going to eat? We're broke, Ted."

About an hour later the conductor returned to the Smoker.

"You can sleep here. Sorry, I can't give you a sleeping berth, but we're full up. Hope you don't mind sitting up?"

"We'd be happy standing on our head all night. We're just glad for the ride to Winnepeg." As he left the Smoker, Ted thanked the conductor who was helping them.

"Now, for some food." Ted left the Smoker and returned an hour later.

"Okay, Jack get ready to sing for your supper while I get my clarinet."

Jack followed Ted down the train car aisle, through the

dinning car that was now vacant, and into the kitchen area where several waiters were eating dinner. He took out his Moose card, showed it to the waiters who also were all Moose, and arranged to entertain them while they ate in exchange for meals while he and Jack were on the train.

"Boys, I'd like you to meet the other half of 'Lewis and Lewis,' my partner, Jack," said Ted when he returned to the dining car with his partner and instruments.

When the waiters heard and saw what "Lewis and Lewis" could do, they clapped, cheered, and shook hands with the entertainers. ""Best meal we've had, ever, with you playing for us," said one of the waiters. "Thanks."

As the waiters left for their sleeping quarters, one of them remained to see that Ted and Jack had all they wanted to eat. For the rest of the trip Jack and Ted entertained the waiters in exchange for their meals.

"We've got to get our money from Happy, Ted said after he and Jack arrived in Winnepeg. Again, Jack waited inside the warm train station while Ted left to send a wire to Harry Rapp, collect. He received no answer.

Ted did not want to wire his parents and let them know he was stranded and needed money. In fact, they did not know where he was or that he was now going under the name of "Ted Lewis." Instead, he decided to go see the manager of the theater where he and Jack played.

When Ted opened the theater manager's office door and walked in, he was amazed at its magnificence.

"May I help you?" Ted looked around the room and saw a receptionist at the far end.

"Yes, thank you." Ted had walked up to a large, dark mahogany desk that held only a telephone, lamp, and pencil holder placed next to an appointment book. The finish of the desk gleamed, matching the warm, dark hair of the attractive young woman sitting behind the desk. "I wish to see the manager, please" said Ted.

"Who is it who wishes to see him?" answered the receptionist.

"I'm with 'Lewis and Lewis.' I'm Ted Lewis and my
partner is Jack Lewis. We played here about three months ago?"
Ted proceeded to tell her the entire story of being stranded
without money in Moose Jaw and having to "beg" their way to
Winnepeg. "I tried wiring my agent in New York for money,
but he didn't answer. Jack and I want to get out of town." Ted
explained that they needed money from the manager for train fare
to Chicago.

"I'm sorry, Mr. Lewis. The manager's not in." The receptionist was silent and looked at Ted Lewis as if expecting him to speak
first. After Ted looked at her for several seconds, she continued.
"I'm very sorry, but I can't do anything for you."

"Well, what are we going to do?" Ted was angry and sat
down in the chair in front of the desk, leaned over it until he
almost touched the face of the receptionist. "Young lady, we've got
money coming to us. We earned it and nobody is paying us. My
agent in New York won't answer my wire."

"Well, I'm sorry. I can't do anything for you now." She
walked to the door and held it open while Ted grudgingly walked
out into the hall. "Goodbye, Mr. Lewis. Please call and make an
appointment before you come again."

Ted was relieved when she closed the door behind him. As
he walk out of the office, he was afraid the receptionist would see
the raccoon coat he carried over one arm as he walked passed her
and down the hall. He hurried out of the building and almost
ran down the street "...before she has a chance to see that vacant
hall tree where this coat was hanging and come after me," he said
to himself. Ted had to find a pawnshop to exchange the coat for
enough money to pay the train fare to take him and Jack back to
Chicago.

Ted was first to lug his worn Candleback trunk into the tiny room at the old Revere House hotel in Chicago where he and Jack were staying. Jack followed, closed the door, and collapsed on the bed. The Revere House was home to many entertainers on the vaudeville circuit and the two felt welcome. Ted slumped into the only chair in the room, Jack sprawled out on one of the beds. Within a few minutes, both were asleep, exhausted from the ordeal of the past few days.

After the last several months of hardship in Canada, both men felt they were now in Paradise. They slept several hours before they awoke to reality in the United States. Their money from the raccoon coat was almost gone and they did not have a job. "At least we're back home," said Jack, his optimism renewed.

Since "Lewis and Lewis" had no booking in Chicago, the two men decided to look separately for temporary work until they could reestablish their act. Ted was first to find a job playing his saxophone at a place on Twenty Second Street while girls hustled customers to drink, earning a percentage from the drinks they sold while Ted entertained.

Jack did not get a job, but in a few weeks he found a girl, left Ted, and the act. He told Ted he was going to get married, stay in Chicago, and find work there.

Once again Ted was alone and discouraged. He felt like a failure in show business. Hopelessly dejected, Ted decided to call Fanny Ward, one of the ladies at Friedman's Bazaar. Miss Ward had taken care of Ted when he was a little boy, and he felt she would understand if he asked her to send him money for a train ticket home.

"Why, of course I'll send the money right away, Teddy," Fanny Ward said, "and I won't tell your parents, either."

When Benjamin and Pauline Friedman saw Ted, they were overjoyed to welcome their son home. This time "...Teddy will surely stay in Circleville and work in our store," said Pauline. Benjamin smiled and agreed.

Once back home, Ted worked only long enough to have

money in his pocket, then left again for New York, this time making sure his parents knew where he would be. He felt more confident than he had in a long time, and knew exactly what he was going to do. He would form his own band as part of a comedy act, and play at Coney Island.

But, first Ted managed to change something else in his life, the unexpected he had not planned.

Chapter Twenty-Six

"Start The Band"

Lights inside the New York burlesque theater dimmed. A red velvet curtain slowly parted. On stage, a spotlight rambled, up, down, and over, searching this entire area outlined by the proscenium arch, a pursuer seeking its pursued. Suddenly, finding its target, it rested upon a worn, vacant cane-back chair at center stage. Those few seconds the chair remained empty seemed an eternity to a full-house audience now making undertones of restless impatience.

One of the curtains, both now pulled to each side of the stage, began to tremble. The audience grew silent. An occasional whisper, followed by a reprimanding, "Hush," from an annoyed theatergoer, was heard. Then, absolute silence as a violin held by an aged hand was extended just outside the drawn curtain. Immediately a bow gripped in the companion hand appeared above the violin.

The face that jerked out from the curtain to join both the violin and its bow was that of an Old Man now caught in the brilliant spotlight that moved from the chair and focused on his entrance. His long, white, tangled hair and rivers of age-spotted wrinkles made him appear more ready for his funeral than to play the instrument held by his shaking hands. Staring out into the black theater, he squinted, then looked in wide-eyed amazement that anyone might be out there in the dark. Apparently satisfied that he did, indeed, have an audience, his body left the curtain sanctuary as he dragged himself, bent and hobbling, to the awaiting chair. He stumbled into the chair with his arms, violin, and bow falling to his sides and his head collapsing onto his rumpled white shirt and torn, black, swallow-tail coat.

From backstage a drum roll sounded, immediately followed by the crash of symbols slammed together. As if awakened from death, the Old Man bolted upright, placed the violin under his chin, and positioned his bow onto the expectant strings. Then, as if he became a young man again, he steadily drew his bow across the violin and began the most beautiful strains of <u>Danny Boy</u> the audience ever heard.

Without stopping, the Old Man finished his piece of music from beginning to end. Immediately he once more began again to play <u>Danny Boy</u>, looking out into the black abyss of the darkened theater and nodding twice, as if recognizing someone in the audience. He played the first line and stopped. After looking out again into the audience and nodding twice, he started over and stopped at the same place as before. Now he looked puzzled, then angry, but resumed his playing for a third time, from the beginning.

"*Oh, Danny Boy,*" began singing a young male voice sounding as if made in heaven, but came from somewhere out in the theater. "*...the pipes, the pipes are calling,...*" it continued from a form now rising slowly out of the theater mid-section. "*...From glen to glen,*" the voice kept on, "*...and from the mountainside....*" The singer was now standing in full view and continuing his song.

The Old Man continued to accompany this "stranger," throwing an occasional questioning glance at the young man, now illumined by house lights and a fickle spotlight that had already abandoned the Old Man and his chair in preference for the singer.

The audience did not seem surprised that someone from the audience was performing. This was common in Burlesque.

It was seldom, however, those watching a performance were moved to tears. When the singer came to the end of the song and finished with, "...*Oh Danny Boy, oh Danny Boy, I love you so*," people jumped from their seats, waved wet handkerchiefs, and were shouting, "More, more." Even the Old Man, as if miraculously recovered from a fatal illness, arose from his chair and ran to the edge of the stage, clapping and grinning, his arms with violin and bow extended high above his head in victory.

Al Jolson, a friend and contemporary of Ted Lewis, had just made his first public appearance. It was in a Burlesque theater when a vocalist and partner of the Old Man failed to appear, and Al Jolson spontaneously decided on his own to take the singer's place and sing Danny Boy. Al Jolson, son of a Jewish Rabbi, had just initiated his career in Burlesque.

Boston, in 1840, was not unlike many of her American sister cities, especially those on or near the East Coast. Huge numbers of immigrants poured onto their soil, refuse from Europe's poverty, looking for economic sanctuary in the United States, finding instead that they were joining the tide of America's nineteenth-century over-expansion woes. Along with everyone else, their battle was with poverty, starvation, and homelessness. Everyone craved some diversion to survive hard times.

This same year, an enterprising Boston saloon owner, eager to increase his dwindling clientele and paltry profits, devised a solution. Was it not possible to draw more people into his saloon if they were entertained while they drank? Some singing and some comedy along with their drinks was the cure, he felt, for his ailing business. Soon he opened the Boston "Vaudeville Saloon," the first Vaudeville variety show in the United States, conceiving the name from an area in France called Val de Vire, and meant "lively songs." Vaudeville was born.

Both Ted Lewis and Al Jolson, along with other entertainers - Milton Beryl, Sophie Tucker, Georgie Price - played in both Vaudeville and Burlesque. By 1915, when Ted Lewis took on another partner, they booked their act in a burlesque show called, "Charlie Robertson's Parisian Flirts" in Rochester, New York. The audience loved them. Not only was the act an important career success for Ted, but his life was about to take on a new dimension.

***

It was 1866 and Lydia Thompson loved performing in Burlesque. She adored everything about the way Burlesque entertained an audience, keeping her fans laughing from the first moment the curtain opened until it closed at the end of the show. It was comedy at its best and she was gloriously happy being part of this entertainment that mimicked reality. "Of course, there are sexual overtones," she thought. "But, isn't that what makes it so much fun for everyone?" She was proud of the way they could poke fun at modern mores, but still remain ladies and present a "good, clean show." They might pretend to take off their clothes. But never, ever, were any of the gorgeous girls performing in Burlesque indecent. It just was not done, on stage or otherwise. "After all, we're nice girls."

"Lydia and Her Bevy of British Blondes" arrived at Wood's Museum at 30th and Broadway and were always greeted with rave reviews wherever they performed. Audiences went wild over Lydia's act which featured four British blondes whose expertise was "The Tease," tempting male members of the audience as they flirted, danced seductively, and satirized sexual mores, especially during one particular show.

The Blondes had just performed their ensemble number, and had retired to their dressing room. Lydia was preparing for her solo that would wind up the show. As Lydia stood in the wings waiting to go on stage, music from the few musicians out front began. She waited until she heard her cue from the music, then, slowly and sensuously Lydia emerged from behind the curtains into full view of a raucous and happy audience, mostly men.

She was dressed in several layers of colorful flowing gowns that covered her beautiful figure, and wore long gloves that everyone knew would soon be shed. Then she would bump and grind and tease back and forth on the stage, occasionally showing a bit of leg here, some shoulder there, never allowing the garment to fall, and keeping her "naughty but nice" demeanor.

Suddenly the music tempo changed to a livelier beat. Lydia became more animated, more mischievous, more seductive as she cavorted across the stage. She took off each glove slowly, playing with it before throwing it into the wings. As she began unfastening her outer gown, ooh's and aah's started coming from the crowd accompanied by an occasional whistle. As she tried to unfasten the last hook, it broke, the entire gown dropped to the floor, and Lydia stood nude before a howling audience. The first strip tease in Burlesque was born.

***

Adah Becker loved show business and was thrilled performing as a dancer in the "Parisian Flirts." It was the dream of a lifetime for the young woman to be dancing on a New York stage, even if it was Burlesque. She knew that some critics considered Burlesque "risqué." Others agreed with her. "After all," Adah said, "Burlesque is just a little bit naughty."

When Adah saw a young clarinet player in a specialty act with the "Parisian Flirts," she hoped that he would notice her. "He's so good looking," she said to another dancer in her act.

"Maybe he'll ask you out," said Adah's friend.

"Wouldn't that be swell?" The two girls hugged each other.

Ted Lewis had noticed the dancer both on stage and off and wondered who she was.

"Her name's Adah Becker," a friend told him. "Pretty cute, eh?"

"You bet she's cute, and pretty good on her feet, too."

"Want me to introduce you to her?"

"I should say so," Ted said. "How about...right now?"

By noon, Ted had met Miss Adah Becker and had a date for dinner with her after the show. Six weeks and three marriage ceremonies later they became Mr. and Mrs. Theodore Leopold Friedman, or Mr. and Mrs. Ted Lewis, on October 7, 1915.

All three "I do's" were repeated on the same day in Rochester, New York. The first was during a civil ceremony at noon in the City Hall. The second was at a Jewish religious ritual rite performed between shows. The third was on stage before friends from the theater, "...and this last stage production of our vows, my friends, was the 'commercial' for our marriage," said Ted whenever he described his wedding day.

They were crazy. There they were, five clowns on a Coney Island stage, each dressed as a Pagliaccho look-a-like. They wore baggy, ruffle-trimmed costumes made of a shiny white fabric emblazoned with large, black circles on an alabaster background. The clowns banged on tin pans, climbed on each others shoulders while playing their instruments, cavorted in and out, over and under whatever was in their way and each other, to whatever Dixieland jazz tunes that caught their fancy as backdrop to their insane antics. Appropriately it was named, "Ted Lewis and His Nut Band."

"I need a new act," Ted told Adah in 1916. After their marriage, she had quit performing to devote her life to her husband's budding career. His comedy acts were drawing raves from those audiences that were accommodated in the small time Vaudeville and Burlesque houses wherever he played. These successes were leading to an occasional Big Time booking with headliners whom he accompanied, such as dancers Bessie Clayton on the Kieth Circuit, and Joan Sawyer at the Aux Caprice room on 59th Street in New York. It was apparent that Ted Lewis was on his way up.

Putting together these five musicians for his "Nut Band"

was only Ted's next step in improving his comedy act, and was not intended to be the start of a formal band. Making his audiences laugh was what Ted loved to do and what drew people to his shows. Along with the laughs, they also got a good introduction to jazz as they listened to those same Dixieland notes and jungle beat that as a kid Ted Friedman had learned from the barbers at Cricket's Barbershop in Circleville.

Between comedy and jazz, it was getting hard to tell which of the two delighted his audience the most. The more raves and enthusiasm he got from these small crowds, more confident he became that humor and jazz were in his blood and the stage was his life. *Goodbye Circleville, Broadway, Hello.*

Chapter Twenty-Seven

"Jungle Blues"

...Boomlay, boomlay, boomlay, Boom,'
A roaring, epic, rag-time tune
From the mouth of the Congo
To the Mountain of the Moon....

...Then I saw the Congo, creeping THROUGH THE BLACK,
CUTTING THROUGH THE FOREST WITH A GOLDEN
TRACK....

...And the crowd in the court gave a whoop and a call
And danced the juba from wall to wall.

Just then from the doorway, as fat as shotes,
Came the cake-walk princes in their long red coats,
Canes with a brilliant lacquer shine,
And tall silk hats that were red as wine.
And they pranced with their butterfly partners there,...

...The cake-walk royalty then began
To walk for a cake that was tall as a man
To the tune of 'Boomlay, boomlay, boomlay, Boom...
*...Walk with care, walk with care,...*Vachel Lindsay / excerpts
from The Congo

Ashanti, inland from the West Coast of Africa, 1619

The Young Tribesman was too slow to out run his captors, the British slave traders. Now the captive, he was packed together with other Ashanti male African youths...a few women were huddled in a tiny corner...in the bottom part of a ship that was tied up to a dock at the port on the West Coast of Africa. He was scared and tears started to run down his face. He quickly wiped them away, afraid others would see his terror and think him a coward. He had to be brave.

The Young Tribesman was one of the stronger Africans who survived the bitter horror of the ship's Atlantic crossing, and was able to walk from the ship. He stepped onto the dock at the British colony of Virginia, and became one of the first Africans to be sold into slavery in North America.

After they arrived, they were auctioned as chattel, bondmen to serve British colonial landowners, slaveholders who bought them as indentured serfs to work in their homes and fields. Now they and their progeny were condemned to slavery for the rest of their lives.

These slaves arrived in the New World with only the clothing they wore when captured, and memories of an Africa they would never see again.

In the sanctuary of his mind, the Young Tribesman treasured the beat and sound of Africa's jungle drums, beating out their measured rhythms. It was the "Boomlay, boomblay, boomblay, Boom," that he worshipped, that struggled for life, but was refused birth by those of the New World who did not understand. It persisted wherever the Tribesman was, in the fields where he worked, in the shack where he ate and slept with the others, and incessant when he was punished.

Other slaves also heard the sounds. When alone together,

they often talked about past celebrations, how they loved to dance and chant to the beat of drums. They missed playing handmade instruments of sound that they blew in unison with the drums, or instruments with strings that they plucked and strummed as the notes and tones blended into the beat...the "Boomlay boom"...of their beloved Africa.

Despite stern dictates of Protestant mores which forbade slaves to make such instruments, pound drums, or chant and dance, the slaves' memories persisted, and Africa's musical heritage, its rhythm, melody, and harmony, would pass on to future generations of the New World.

Three centuries after the British introduced slavery to Virginia, a new kind of music that was bred and born of the Congo, found itself nurtured and developed within the freedom allowed only by the United States. It would grow, mature, and sweep the country with its untamed rhythm, harmony, and melody, eventually changing forever the face and future of music throughout the world.

They called it...**Jazz!**

Chapter Twenty-Eight

"In The Land of Jazz"

Competition was fierce. In 1917, up scale New York restaurants like Reisenwebers, at 981 Eighth Street, did everything possible to have the best food, dance floor, service, and entertainment in order to attract the wealthiest and largest number of patrons in New York City. Reisenwebers succeeded after it hired the Original Dixieland Jazz Band whose first ever recording of jazz became popular. After the recording became successful, the five-man band was better known as ODJB. Its five musicians were: cornetist Dominic ("Nick") James LaRocca, clarinetist Larry Shields, trombonist Edwin ("Eddie") Broadford Edwards, pianist Harry W. Ragas, and drummer, Anthony ("Tony") Sbaarbaro. They were all white males and first became known in New Orleans where Dixie Land thrived. This first recording of jazz started a craze that reached across the continent.

Rumors about the demand for these new jazz sounds were already circulating among theater moguls, and those who ran Reisenwebers were the first to take advantage of its popularity. They hoped ODJB with its jazz would entice the public to forsake other restaurants in New York and come to theirs. They were right. The band, and its original recording, had created a demand for jazz beyond what Reisenwebers expected. New customers wanting to hear more of this new sound, jazz, were lined up at the door.

Rectors, a rival of Reisenwebers, and one of the largest restaurants in New York, was at Broadway and Forty-eighth Street. It was loosing business to Reisenwebers because so many people wanted to see the popular OBJB band and hear this new jazz that they played. Its owner, George Rector, was determined to bring back his customers. Rectors, he planned, would hire a band that played even better jazz than ODJB. If Rectors could attract the demanding 250-pound, railroad magnate, Diamond Jim Brady, often accompanied by singer-actress Lillian Russell on his arm, he could do anything. George Rector laughed when he thought of those early nineteen hundreds when he welcomed Diamond Jim and Miss Russell at the front door with the greeting, "Here comes my twenty-five best customers." Diamond Jim, who would eat dozens of Blue Point oysters at one siting, followed by a dozen crabs, several bowls of turtle soup, duck, steak, several varieties of lobster plus vegetables, pastries, and several pounds of chocolate, died that year in 1917. George Rector would miss his favorite customer. He could not afford to lose any more.

"Ted," said George Rector, "I need a band that plays jazz. Can you get one together and work for me? It has to be better than ODJB"

Ted Lewis was now at The Aux Caprice Domino Room, atop Pestonomy's New York restaurant. He played clarinet with pianist Earl Fuller and his Fuller's Famous Jazz Band, and Ted was beginning to be popular as an entertainer and musician. He grinned. "You bet I can, George. Give me a couple of months and I'll be there with my band."

"Make it sooner. I need you."

Both men left smiling. George Rector returned to Rectors restaurant, hopeful of regaining his errant customers, and Ted Lewis went back to play in Fuller's jazz band until he formed his own, Fuller retaining certain rights to his performances at Rectors. *This is what I've been waiting for. Have a new act. Form a new band. New York, just wait 'til you see what I've got for you.*

Ted and his new band not only gave Rectors' audience the Jazz George Rector sought, but also sights and sounds it never heard before. The trombones laughed, clarinets sobbed, and hat-muted instruments, with their "wah-wah-wah's," talked to an audience that seemed to understand every word and sentiment coming from each instrument. The antics of Ted Lewis on stage were wild and crazy, and his "gas pipe" clarinet style of "... blowing and creating a shrill sound that was useful on novelty tunes but frowned on by most players in most settings..." drove the audience into hysteria. It stomped, hollered, and cheered when the show ended. Ted Lewis and His Band were a hit, and Rectors reclaimed its clientele. After a few months of continued success, George Rector felt he had won his competition battle with Reisenwebers, and Ted Lewis became known as "The Jazz King."

Mississippi's Hansome Cab was made for romance. The two-wheeled, one horse dawn carriage was made with the driver's seat elevated at the rear, and was above and beyond the cab, which could be covered for additional privacy should the couple in love who were riding in it so desire. Mississippi, a former prizefighter, drove the young lovers all around Central Park for as long as they wished without him seeing them, or they seeing him. Naturally, the longer the drive, the more money he made, both in fares and in tips. "I like the long ones," Mississippi would say to himself," then laugh out loud at his joke, secretly hoping no customers were near enough to hear. He loved his job and would never offend anyone. Mississippi became famous among these cab drivers after Damon Runyon, well-known journalist, had written about him. He had to live up to his good reputation.

Tonight Ted Lewis was eager for the intermission during the band's nighttime performance. During the break, Ted went outside Rectors to where the Hansome cabs were parked, and where he enjoyed talking to the cabbies. Mississippi was his favorite, especially after reading the newspaper article his friend, Damon Runyon, wrote about him. When he got outside, he looked for Mississippi, but he could not find him in his usual spot.

"Hey, Mister Lewis. Over here."

Ted looked around until he found from where the familiar voice came.

"Mississippi, how come you're parked over there?" he called.

"Only place left for my cab, Mr. Lewis. Come on up. There's plenty of room." Mississippi moved over as Ted climbed up and sat next to him. "How's everything goin' for you?"

"Great, Mississippi. A little tired tonight. But, like I told you, I love every minute of it. How about you?"

"Fine, Mr. Lewis, just fine."

"Miss, I've been meaning to ask you about that hat you've got on. Are you ever going to get a new one?"

Mississippi laughed. "I guess I'd better before this one wears out and falls off my head. Things have been pretty good lately, Mr. Lewis, so I was thinkin' of gettin' a new one. Just need to make a little more money first."

"Good idea, Miss. But, what are you going to do with this old one?

"This old thing? Don't know, Mr. Lewis, guess I'll throw it away. Not much good anymore."

"Tell you what, Mississippi. You need a little more loot, and I need something new for my act. How about your hat?"

Mississippi looked puzzled, then said, "You want this old thing...why?"

"Don't know. Just got a feeling."

Both men were silent. Ted Lewis spoke first.

"Mississippi, I've got a pair of dice in my pocket." He reached into one of them and pulled out a pair of ivory dice with black dots. "I'll tell you what I'll do. I'll shoot you a quarter against your old hat."

"Okay, Mr. Lewis, if you're sure you want this battered up, old hat." Mississippi shot the dice, two sixes came up, and he looked at Ted Lewis.

"Well, Mississippi, that's crap. You lose. I win."

Ted Lewis gave Mississipi the quarter, the cab driver gave him his hat, and Ted Lewis went back upstairs to finish the band's evening performance.

As he joined the waiting band, he waved his new, old battered hat with one hand high above his head. Slowly, he walked to center stage where he stopped. He stood for a few seconds, looking out into the hushed audience. Then he raised his other arm and took the other edge of the hat's brim into that hand, and held it high above his head. Now in both hands, he lowered the hat onto his head, giving it a slight tilt as a final adjustment before removing his hands and lowering his arms to his side. When he smiled and gave a final tap to the hat with a snap of his fingers, the audience became alive and wild with applause and cheers.

Well, Mississippi, what do you think of your beat up hat now that it's part of show business?

As 1917 advanced towards 1918, Ted Lewis felt something must be wrong with his performance. Rectors and his popularity were growing. But, the audience seemed different, more subdued, and he wondered if he needed to change his act.

"Absolutely not," said George Rector. "It's not you, Ted, or your band. Everyone loves what you're doing. The country is worried about our getting involved in this World War. Your audience is just glum. Ted, keep up what your doing and they'll come around."

Ted still wasn't convinced. *I've got to do something to cheer them up. World War or not, I've got to find something to make them happy when they're watching my show.* Ted spent the next few weeks trying to figure out how he could do it. Sometimes during his performances that followed, the crowd seemed its old self, jubilant and receptive to his act. Other times, Ted Lewis noticed the audience return to an aura of gloom. He felt his own enthusiasm on stage reflect the mood of his audience. Ted Lewis needed everyone, including himself, to be happy if he was to give a good show.

One day when news of the warfront was discouraging, United States troops had suffered a set back, and his nighttime audience was even more unresponsive than usual. Something had to be done.

When his show was almost over, and the patrons left their tables for the last dance of the evening, Ted suddenly stopped the band. For a moment Ted and the dancers just looked at each other. Then, as if it had always been part of his act, Ted Lewis took off his hat, waved it in the air, and said, "Is everybody happy?"

The house came down with screams from the audience of "Yes," "You bet we're happy," and "Swell, Ted, we're with you."

With three little words that he spoke to cheer up an anxious audience during troubled times, Ted Lewis added a new dimension to his show. "Is everybody happy?' was now a permanent part of his performance.

During the coming year of 1918, he not only worked at Rectors, but also for World War One causes by visiting hospitals and camps all over the country. He sold United States bonds to Americans, many who came just to hear him ask this question that was now part of his trademark as it joined his battered hat, twirling black cane, and his clarinet. He always made sure each of these was included in his show. *That's what the people come to see and hear, and that's what you give them.* Ted Lewis was convinced that success came from great showmanship. The performer, he believed, must know what the public wants and then make sure it gets it. Ted Lewis made sure his public got what it wanted.

This increasing showmanship and popularity now pushed him towards celebrity. After he made his first recording for Columbia Records in October of this same year, and the public could purchase a single 78 RPM record of Ted Lewis singing, <u>Wond'ring</u> and <u>Blues My Naughty Sweetie Gave To Me</u>, he earned fame.

Ted Lewis had come a long way from sweeping floors at Friedman's Bazaar in Circleville, Ohio, a job he hated only because he loved show business so much. When on stage, he always showed his genuine love for his family and hometown. It was a vital part of his act for him to tell his audiences that, "Circleville is the Capitol of the world," and was almost as familiar to them as, "Is everybody happy?" All these elements the audience came to see, combined as his trademark and his on-stage signature. Ted Lewis and those he entertained demanded them all.

The Jazz King made sure no one was ever disappointed.

Chapter Twenty-Nine

"Wear a Hat With a Silver Lining"

One thing John Murray Anderson knew for sure. He excelled at producing musical shows.

"He's the best," said Phillip Bartholomae who wrote the book for his production, The Greenwich Village Follies of 1919.

"There's no one better," said Arthur Swanstrom who was currently working with him on the lyrics for the prospective The Greenwich Follies of 1920.

"It's a real privilege to be in one of his shows," said Ivan Bancroft who was one of the entertainers being considered for the Follies, along with other performers like Margaret Davies and Pee Wee Meyers, who agreed with his opinion of Murray Anderson. They all found him strict, but fair, and respected his artistic judgement.

"How'd you like a spot in the Follies, Ted?" Murray Anderson had just congratulated Ted Lewis on his performance at Rectors. He always kept his professional eye open to newcomers on New York's entertainment scene. Ted Lewis had caught that eye and Murray was sure Ted would be a smash in one of his productions.

"I'd love it, Mr. Anderson," said Ted when Murray asked him to join his show.

"Murray, Ted. Call me Murray. We've got a new change of

scenery planned over at the Follies and need an act to fill in while we make it. How's that sound?"

"Great, sir...Murray. When can I start?"

"But Ted," said Adah when her husband told her about accepting the offer from Murray Anderson, "how in the world are you going to manage two separate shows at the same time? "

Ted smiled, kissed Adah, and said, "Don't know, Sweetheart, but I will."

A week later, Ted Lewis and his Jazz Band were performing in The Greenwich Follies of 1919, and their audiences heard for the first time hat-muted sounds that seemed impossible to come from musical instruments. Each one sounded almost human as the trombone laughed, then the cornet laughed back, and when the clarinet laughed at both the trombone and cornet, it stopped the show. By the next day, Ted Lewis and his band were the stars of the Follies. Murray Anderson had scored another hit.

"My Ziegfeld Follies features the most beautiful girls in the world. There's not an ugly one among them," boasted Florenz Ziegfeld, more intimately called Flo or Ziggy to those who knew him. Each night he proved his statement as these ravishing young women were put on display wearing stunning costumes, and stood poised atop a high-rise stairway that covered most of the stage of Ziegfeld's New Amsterdam Theater, every beautiful face framed by a sunburst headdress, often made of artfully blended colorful feathers. Each showgirl wore a unique and individually styled costume, ornate but tasteful, and scant enough to reveal most of her tall, statuesque and flawless body. Before she began her descent, she would pose for the audience, then begin her way down each step, slowly and regally, to the strains of an appropriate song, often the popular <u>A Pretty Girl is Like a Melody.</u>

Flo Ziegfeld was a master showman who knew that talent as well as beauty was necessary to attract an audience, and sought out exceptional entertainers such as Fanny Brice singing, <u>Ten Little Indians</u> and <u>Second Hand Rose</u>, W. C. Fields, and Will

Rogers.

When Ziegfeld decided to follow Hammerstien's decision to attract a summer crowd with an evening cooled roof garden atop his Victoria Theater, Ziggy built his own roof garden, The Midnight Frolics. He hoped to include the famous Ted Lewis who accepted immediately when Flo Ziegfeld offered him and his band the chance to play for late night dancing and entertainment.

When her husband told Adah Lewis of this new booking, she knew it was useless to ask Ted how he would manage performing in three separate shows - Rectors, The Follies of 1919, and Ziegfeld's Midnight Frolics - in three different places at the same time. She already knew the answer. *But, please dear God, don't let there be a number four.*

After Benjamin Franklin Keith created his vaudeville circuit in 1880 by opening several theaters for vaudeville artists in which to perform, his theaters grew in number for many years. After his death in 1914, the B.F. Keith circuit continued to thrive by booking vaudeville acts regularly into its several hundred theaters throughout the country, playing his Palace Theater in New York being every vaudevillian's goal and symbol of success. When Ted Lewis signed his contract to play the Palace, he fulfilled his own life-long dream.

In 1919, the Shuberts of the Sam S. Subert Theater in Boston decided to revive "The Passing Show," the first truly American musical review to be produced and presented to audiences in 1894. For the new "Passing Show," an update of the old review, the Shuberts wanted Ted Lewis who now was in constant demand throughout the Big Time houses and clubs. After "The Passing Show," Ted returned to Greenwich Village to perform in the "Greenwich Follies of 1920, " 1921, and 1922, the Bal Tabarin, the Montmarte, and at his own Ted Lewis Club at 52nd and 7th Avenue. After he failed financially as a club owner, he was convinced of two things. First, he would concentrate on bookings with other theaters, clubs, and circuits. Second, and equally important, Adah would assume full management of his career. Subsequent bookings with West Coast vaudeville theaters then took him to San Francisco and Los Angeles where the Orpheum was the major vaudeville circuit.

After returning to the East Coast with appearances in several productions, including "Artists and Models," and "La Maires Affairs," he received a call from The Ambassador Hotel near Beverly Hills in Los Angeles.

"Ted, this is Abe Frank. Remember me, the manager at the Coconut Grove? Are you planning to come back to LA soon?"

"Of course I remember you, Abe. Why?"

"Well, I need someone for the Grove, and I was hoping to get you, Ted."

Ted Lewis thought for a few seconds.

"Ted, are you there?"

"Sure, Abe, just thinking. You know, it just might work out. I've got some personal business in Hollywood and I'd love to play the Grove. Got a date in mind?"

As Ted Lewis walked through the famous Moroccan style doors that led into the Ambassador's Coconut Grove, he was early for his first nightly show back at the Grove. *This has to be the most beautiful club entrance I've ever seen.* As he looked at the gold leaf and palm trees etched into the glass doors, he thought of the thousands of people who had entered through them since the Grove opened on April 21, 1921. Tonight, he thought, thirteen hundred more will jam the seats and balconies, fill the Grove to capacity, and experience the ambiance and quality entertainment of one of the most lush and unique nightclubs in the world. Once inside, they would also discover why it was aptly named The Coconut Grove.

Its predecessor, and first Los Angeles nightclub, had opened several months before the Grove as "The Zinnia Grill," its name due to the Zinnias that were lavishly painted on its décor of black polished satin, often referred to as "The Black Patent Leather

Room." The Zinnia Grill was located on the Casino level below the hotel in the deep recesses of the Ambassador. As its popularity among city officials and Hollywood's early film personalities exploded, the now too-small Zinnia Room was replaced by a larger Grand Ballroom and converted into a first-class nightclub, The Coconut Grove.

These lower regions of the Ambassador were the perfect setting for a prestigious nightclub, meticulously planned to cater, not only to city officials and filmdom's elite, but also to the wealthy and socially prominent of Los Angeles. These celebrities coveted the free publicity from their grand entrance that they made on the arm of one of the captains, or maitré d, as each one descended like royalty down an exquisite staircase before escorted to a private, reserved table.

Rudolph Valentino, renowned lover and heartthrob of silent films, was responsible for the name as well as the interior setting of the Grove. In 1921, having just completed his most famous movie, "The Sheik," Valentino suggested that the desert setting constructed for the film, now abandoned on the beaches of Oxnard, California some seventy miles north of Hollywood, be used as décor for the Grove. Valentino's offer was accepted, and the rescued remains of Rudolph Valentino's film now transformed the old Grand Ballroom into an island paradise of coconut trees made of paper maché with palm fronds covering the entire ceiling, and stuffed monkeys, with blinking electric amber eyes, swinging from tree to tree. In a painted blue ceiling sky overhead, stars also twinkled electrically, while a tapestry covering on one wall depicted a huge Hawaiian moon shinning on a painted landscape, with an actual waterfall cascading, then splashing into a pool below.

Seeing old friends was an added perk for Ted whenever he played the Grove. During tonight's intermission he would "table-hop" and renew old acquaintances.

All eyes were focused on the blond beauty now posed atop

the Grove stairway. The movie star was dressed in a long, black velvet evening gown trimmed with white fox that encircled its low cut bodice in the front, as well as its long, extended train in the back. As its white fox edged train trailed down the stairs behind the French-designed creation she wore, seductively it emphasized the full, exquisite figure of Mae West who made her grand entrance down the staircase on the arm of the maitré d, slowly escorting her to her table. Enhancing the drama and attention drawn to her, Miss West stood a few seconds before allowing a waiter to seat her. Tonight she was alone, not uncommon for one of the glamour queens of Hollywood who occasionally appeared in public fashionably unescorted. It was intermission, and when she saw Ted Lewis seated with George Burns and his wife, Gracie Allen, she blew the bandleader a kiss with one of her long black gloved hands.

Ted excused himself from his friend's table, telling George Burns that he'd call him while he was in town, and went over to Mae West's table.

"Mae, you look absolutely gorgeous," Ted said, kissing her cheek, then sitting down in the chair across from her.

"Thanks, Teddy, just a little item I had hanging in my closet. Like the Tiffany's brooch?" she asked caressing a magnificent diamond creation pinned on the gown, but partly resting on her cleavage. "How's Adah?"

"Just fine, Mae. She'll be here one of these nights. She'd love to see you."

They talked a few minutes more when Ted excused himself.

"I see Charlie Chaplin over there and want to say hello before the show starts again."

Ted walked over to Chaplin's table where he was sitting with Gloria Swanson and Marion Davies.

"Charlie," Ted said as he shook Chaplin's hand, "How are you?"

Chaplin introduced Ted to his two companions, who both

complemented Ted on his show. "I just loved it," said Gloria Swanson. Marion Davies giggled and added, "Me, too."

Ted thanked them both as he was leaving to go back on stage, then turned to Chaplin. "Charlie, what do you think about the talkies by now?"

"This is how I see it, Ted. The Little Tramp will never speak, and he's not through making pictures yet."

Ted said goodbye to the three stars, then returned to finish his show.

Later, when Ted Lewis played his final performance at the Grove and was preparing to return to New York, Abe Frank called him into his office.

"Ted," Frank said, "just thought you'd like to know. Your show's been one of the most popular we've ever had. In fact, Ted, you hold the record for attendance at the Grove." Abe Frank went over to shake his hand. "Thanks, Ted, and don't forget. You're welcome back anytime. How about early fall?"

During the decade, Ted Lewis was proclaimed the highest paid performer in the business. Since 1919, when he made his first electrical 78 RPM record, Wond'ring on one side, and Blues My Naughty Sweetie Gave to Me on the other, for the infant Columbia Recording Company, his record sales soared, as did his fame and wealth. When he later recorded for Mercury, Decca, and RKO Unique, his records sold records in the millions. In 1926, Tiger Rag sold five and a half million copies. Others included Some of These Days, with vocal by his close friend, Sophie Tucker, Three O'clock in the Morning, Alexander's Ragtime Band, When My Baby Smiles at Me, I'm Walking Around in a Dream, and I'm the Medicine Man For Your Blues. He became Columbia's highest paid and top recording artist. The company awarded him with the only record label ever designed for a performer at that time, a silver label bearing his picture.

Ted Lewis was now one of the most sought after entertainers in the United States, Europe, and Canada. In England he

Ted Lewis and his "Shadow." Courtesy: Photofest.

answered a Command Performance at the British palace before the King and his son, the Prince of Wales. While in London, he appeared at the Kit Kat Restaurant, Hippodrome, and Piccadilly Revels. His battered hat, wailing clarinet, and twirling cane became his internationally recognized trademark.

At home Ted Lewis was a favorite at the White House, giving Command Performances for several presidents. Wherever he played, audiences packed into theaters to hear his, "Yes sir," clarinet and infectious whistling, and "Is everybody happy?" After he adopted, <u>When My Baby Smiles At Me</u>, as his theme song, his popularity rose even higher and on to new heights. There was no doubt that Ted Lewis was now the crowned "High Hatted Tragedian of Song," "Pied Piper of Happiness," "The Medicine Man for Your Blues." and reigned as "The Jazz King."

It was in 1925 when everyone went wild the first time they heard Ted Lewis sing his new song, <u>Me and My Shadow</u>, on stage, and had his own shadow thrown up on a shadow box behind him. Audiences were spellbound as they watched the shadow follow him with dancing hands and twirling cane that were identical to his own movements as he strolled in front of his audience, talking and singing the words until he reached the far end of the stage.

During one of his performances, Ted noticed there was something going on towards the back of the theater while he sang, Me and My Shadow. Very interesting, he thought.

At intermission, instead of going on a break he walked to the back of the theater, to the surprise of those milling about the foyer. He walked up to a short, pleasant looking usher who beamed when he saw Ted Lewis coming towards him.

"Mr. Lewis, what...I mean, can I do something for you?"

"Well, young man, maybe you can. What's your name?"

"Eddie, Sir. Eddie Chester."

"Eddie. That's a fine name. Now, Eddie, tell me, what is it you were doing while I was singing, <u>Me and My Shadow</u>?"

***Ted Lewis and one of his several "shadows" perform
<u>"Me and My Shadow."</u>***

The usher looked stunned. "Oh, Mr. Lewis. I didn't mean for you to see me. I didn't mean to interrupt..."

"No, no, Son. You didn't do anything wrong. Not at all. In fact, I was fascinated by the way you were imitating my movements during <u>Me and My Shadow</u>."

"Mr. Lewis. I'm really sorry if I..."

"Eddie, you didn't interrupt. In fact, you gave me a wonderful idea. Have you memorized the moves I make to <u>Me and My Shadow</u>?"

"Every one, Sir." Eddie grinned.

"Can you do them without looking at me?"

"Oh, I do it all the time when I'm by myself."

"Good, Eddie. Meet me here tomorrow night one hour early. Let's see what kind of a shadow you'd make."

The next night, when Ted Lewis sang <u>Me and My Shadow</u>, a young man, whom no one in the audience recognized, was following him. Wearing a top hat and carrying a cane, he was walking behind Ted Lewis. It was Eddie Chester, whose own shadow now followed behind the shadow of Ted Lewis. Both men were moving in perfect sync as the shadow of each appeared, duplicating their movements on the shadow box.

This new version of <u>Me and My Shadow</u> was a sensation. The audience clapped and cheered so long and hard that Ted and Eddie could not leave. Finally, Ted walked to the edge of the stage, looked out into the theater as if personally greeting each one there, and said, "Let me introduce someone to you. Folks, I'd like you to meet Eddie Chester, my new shadow. You'll be seeing a lot of him from now on. My friends, is everybody happy, now?" Both he and Eddie took a bow in front of a roaring crowd, walked off the stage together, waving and smiling to a cheering audience.

Nor could Ted Lewis be happier at the end of the song as Eddie Chester and he stepped from the stage and into the theater wing. He felt that <u>Me and My Shadow,</u> with the addition of a

*Picture from the files of Academy of Motion Picture
Arts and Sciences.*

real shadow, was the essential final ingredient needed to complete his act that had been in the making for the past ten years. His professional trademark and signature were now complete.

***

Adah could hardly wait to tell Ted the good news. As soon as she heard the front door open, she ran to greet him as he closed the door behind him.

"Oh, Ted, we got the most wonderful phone call today. Warner Brothers wants you in Hollywood by June to start making pictures. And they want you to write a script about your life and bring it with you. I told them I was sure you'd do it." Adah stopped talking, her smile vanished, and she frowned. "You will do it, won't you, Ted?"

Adah made all the arrangements, which included a booking at the Palace Theater in downtown Los Angeles. Ted insisted that there be work for him in case the movies did not work out. It was only 1928, and Jolson's talking movie, "The Jazz Singer," was considered by many to be a novelty that would not last. Ted's own "wait and see" attitude made him cautious. The Palace booking was his insurance in case his own movie did not go over.

He arrived in Hollywood by train. Adah would follow after she got things in order in New York. Both of them were happy and excited about this new venture in Ted's career.

When Ted Lewis took his script to show the writers at their first meeting, Ted Lewis asked them why they hired him for the movies.

"Ted," the writer who seemed to be in charge answered, "we think talking pictures will be more in demand than we thought. We have to be ready to supply the public with what it wants.

"Right now, Hollywood has a problem. A lot of silent film stars just aren't going to make it. I'm talking now about the transition from the silents to sound. Some of these movie stars have awful voices. Ye gods, Ted, you ought to hear Mary Pickford in sound. Pitiful, just pitiful. Others are terrible actors and actresses when they have to talk. And forget about learning dialogue. Some can't memorize anything more than the alphabet. A few will adapt just fine. We already know how you, and Jolson, and Cantor sound and what you all are capable of doing. That's why we're bringing people like you to Hollywood.

"In a nutshell, Ted, we have to get entertainers like you three who have all the necessary talents to make good sound pictures. You all sing, or make music in one way or the other. And you can act. Singing, Ted, is nothing more than acting set to music. Sound is here to stay, and you're going to be an important part of it.

"Now, let's see this script you brought along."

When the writers called Ted back a few days later, they looked more serious than at their first meeting.

"Ted, your script is very interesting, especially about your mother and father being Jewish immigrants from Europe. Obviously you are very proud of your parents' store, and also your hometown...what was that name?"

"Circleville, Ohio," said Ted. "It's the capitol of the world, Gentlemen."

"Of course, Ted. But, we have a couple of ideas and, well, we're sure you're going to agree with them after you hear us out.

"Now look, Ted, we don't think you ought to come from Circleville, Ohio, because Circleville has no color."

"No color?" he said, incensed at this defamation of his hometown. "Evidently none of you has ever been in Circleville. Circleville, Ohio, my friends, has everything."

"Ted, I'm sure that's true. But, this is how we'd like to change it, just a little bit, of course.

"We think you should come from a beautiful southern town, Atlanta, maybe? Your mother should be a lovely, gracious southern belle. We see your father as a true southern gentleman

175

Ted Lewis, "The Jazz King," and Sophie Tucker, " The Last of the Red Hot Mamas," combine talents as they perform one of their famous routines for radio. Courtesy of the Ted Lewis Museum.

Special Material   'For Ted Lewis - Sophie Tucker
by Mac Maurada   July 29, 1959

-1-

LEWIS - TUCKER ROUTINE

FOLLOWING TUCKER SPOT:

LEWIS.... YOU'RE WONDERFUL, SOPHIE, JUST WONDERFUL.

TUCKER... THANKS TED. THE FEELING IS MUTUAL. IN FACT
          YOU ARE MY FAVORITE ~~HEBREW~~

LEWIS.... YOU MEAN THERE ARE OTHERS?

TUCKER... SURE. THERE'S JERRY LEWIS....JOE E. LEWIS....AND
          JOHN L. LEWIS.

LEWIS.... I'VE HEARD OF JERRY AND JOE E. BUT WHAT DOES
          JOHN L. DO?

TUCKER... HE RAISES EYEBROWS.

LEWIS.... ~~XXXX~~ WE'VE RAISED A FEW OURSELVES IN DAYS GONE BY,
          HAVEN'T WE SOPH?

TUCKER... I'LL SAY WE HAVE.

LEWIS.... YEAH. BACK IN 1916 B.A.

TUCKER... B.A. ?

LEWIS.... DO YOU KNOW THAT WHEN THEY TOLD ME THAT SOPHIE TUCKER WOULD BE
          ON THE BILL WITH ME, I THOUGHT I'D BE WORKING WITH
          YOUR DAUGHTER.

TUCKER... AND I THOUGHT I'D BE WORKING WITH TED LEWIS
          THE THIRD.

TED..... YOU KNOW HOW IT IS, SOPH. YOU LOSE TRACK OF PEOPLE
          THRU THE YEARS. RIGHT?

TUCKER... RIGHT. BY THE WAY....WHATEVER BECAME OF YOU?

LEWIS.... I'VE BEEN AROUND. ITS YOU WHO DROPPED OUT OF SIGHT.

TUCKER... ME DROP OUT OF SIGHT. THAT'S LIKE LOSING AN
          ELEPHANT IN SCHWABS DRUG STORE.

page 2

LEWIS....'. I'M ONLY KIDDING SOPH. I KNOW WHAT A BIG
SUCCESS YOU'VE BEEN EVERYWHERE....BIGGER AND
BETTER THAN EVER.

TUCKER... AND I FOLLOW YOUR CAREER TOO, TED. YOU'RE STILL
MISTER SHOW BUSINESS.

IF YOU'LL EXCUSE ME NOW

WHILE I MAKE A LITTLE CHANGE

I'LL BE BACK LATER.

TED...... WHAT ARE YOU GOING TO DO?

TUCKER... MAKE A LITTLE CHANGE.

LEWIS.... AT YOUR AGE?
DON'T FORGET THE GREEN STAMPS.

<u>EXIT</u>

There goes America's answer to Doctor Strange Love!

Above and prior page - An edited radio script of one the many radio routines performed by Ted Lewis and Sophie Tucker. Courtesy of the Ted Lewis Museum.

and a great follower of Lee. Doesn't that sound great?"

"No, I'm sorry, it doesn't sound good to me at all. My mother was never a southern belle. As for my father, the only Lee that he would have followed was Gypsy Rose Lee," he said after naming the famous strip tease artist.

When Adah arrived in Los Angeles, she was anxious to hear every detail of her husband's new movie career.

"Adah, my dear, let me put it to you this way. How would you like to have a mother-in-law who speaks with a southern accent, and attends the Baptist church on Sunday instead of her Jewish Temple on Saturday?"

***

In early fall of 1928, when Ted Lewis returned to the Coconut Grove, its thirteen hundred-seat room was again overflowing with fans that wanted to see the same show they always expected from Ted Lewis, except for a few new specialty acts that were always part of his act. Ted Lewis always said that his secret to his popularity and success "...is in great measure showmanship...." He made sure he followed his own advice as the five-foot, six-inch, 143 pound bowlegged entertainer, whose dark, curly hair was covered by an old battered and worn out black top hat, sauntered, cavorted, or strutted across the stage holding a walking stick, or clarinet, or both. His audiences knew that his musical messages of love and happiness were meant just for them.

Ted Lewis also knew that new entertainers in show business had to know what not to do and when not to do it. "You have to be discovered doing what you should be doing, just when you should be doing it." Then he added, "The theatrical Balboas had better be near when you're doing what you should be doing, if you're going to make good."

Ted Lewis also knew that his audiences expected and demanded quality from his show. He made sure they got it,

*Ted Lewis, Lou Costello, and Bud Abbot, from the movie,
"Hold That Ghost." Courtesy Photofest.*

*"Buck Privates" (1941) was Abbot and Costello's first starring
vehicle, a surprise hit. Before its release, their second, a haunted
house comedy, had been completed as a B picture called, " Oh
Charlie!" However, another armed services musical comedy, "In
The Navy," was rushed into release as followup. "Oh Charlie!"
was renamed, " Hold That Ghost," becoming Abbot and Costello's
third picture as stars, and was beefed up to an "A" of 86 minutes
by adding the Andrew Sisters, and Ted Lewis and His Orchestra
in the opening and closing nightclub segments. Courtesy of Eric,
Spiker, Photofest.*

Ted Lewis with the beautiful dancers who appear with in his "Your My Thrill" number in Metro Goldwyn Mayer's " Here Comes the Band," directed by Paul Sloane.
Courtesy of Clarence Sinclair Bull.

Ted Lewis with the beautiful dancers who appear with in his "Your My Thrill" number in Metro Goldwyn Mayer's " Here Comes the Band," directed by Paul Sloane.
Courtesy of Clarence Sinclair Bull.

Ted Lewis in first movie, 1929, "Is Everybody Happy?", with Ann Pennington, Courtesy Photofest.

Spanky McFarland, diminutive "Our Gang" comedian, taking a clarinet lesson from Ted Lewis. Spanky and Ted appear together in a musical number from one of the Metro-Goldwyn-Mayer productions, "Here Comes The Band." Courtesy Photofest.

Ted Lewis and his band in movie night club performances.
Source Unknown.

especially in his musicians, and he hired only the best of the profession. Some of these men were Muggsy Spanier on trumpet, clarinet and saxaphone man, Don Murray, replaced after his death by Frank Teschmacher. Other artists were trombonist George Brunies, and Frank Ross on piano. Jimmy Dorsey, already a widely recognized clarinetist, brought a new dimension to the band. Later he was replaced by the promising clarinetist Benny Goodman, whose first recording with the Ted Lewis band in 1931 was the successful <u>Dip Your Brush in the Sunshine</u>, which featured the 21-year-old clarinet player and Muggsy Spanier on trumpet, Paul Whiteman, and Walter Kahn. Ted Lewis was a demanding bandleader and perfectionist, ridged and unyielding about every rule that he imposed upon them and himself. Despite an occasional complaint that he was "...too strict...," most band members felt they were well paid, respected their leader's professionalism, even approving of his constant demand for perfection. They knew that Ted Lewis required even tougher standards for himself.

After his last appearance at the Coconut Grove, there was a silent absence of Ted Lewis for over a year and a half of his career between the years of 1929 and 1931, until his band reassembled again in 1932 with a few changes, including Benny Goodman replacing Jimmy Dorsey on clarinet. During this hiatus, Ted Lewis disappeared from the entertainment scene. Those most concerned with his career were told that Adah Lewis was seriously ill, and that Ted Lewis has vowed to remain by her side and care for her until she was completely well.

In 1932, Ted and Adah Lewis moved into their new apartment at 115 Central Park West in New York City that overlooked Central Park. After the void from 1928 and 1932, Ted's professional life resumed, once again managed by Adah Lewis, and was as successful as ever.

Ted Lewis and his wife, Adah Becker Lewis.
Courtesy Photofest.

Chapter Thirty

"Some of These Days"

Edward R. Murrow sat back in his chair, smoking a cigarette as the television camera for his weekly "Person to Person" program zoomed in for a close-up of the famous journalist now-turned TV host. He was interviewing one of the most famous men in the entertainment industry.

"I don't think," he said, "Ted Lewis has ever played opera. But, if there is any other brand of show business he's missed, I'm certain he's ready at the drop of his battered hat to give it a try. For more than 45 years Ted Lewis, his hat, and his clarinet have been asking America, "Is everybody happy?" and telling us about When My Baby Smiles at Me, and Me and My Shadow. In all that time, all he has changed is his tuxedo."

Murrow turned to Ted. "Well, I know you're never at a loss for something to do. What's the latest Ted Lewis enterprise?"

Ted Lewis inched forward towards the edge of the couch where he was sitting in the living room of his New York apartment overlooking Central Park. He was animated, enthusiastic, and appeared to be enjoying every minute of this interview with Ed Murrow.

"Well, they're going to make my life story for the third time in pictures. You know, Ed, they made two others. In fact, before I finish, I think it's going to be a serial."

The Lewises attend a private party: Row 1, left to right are Ted Lewis, Sara Weintraub, unidenitified, Ada Lewis, and Milton Weintraub. Back row, both unidentified.
Courtesy of Sara Weintraub.

Ted was grateful that Murrow made no mention of his radio career. He never really liked doing radio and was glad he did not have to talk about it now on Murrow's show. Throughout the Thirties and Forties, Ted Lewis headlined popular radio shows which included "Coca Cola Spotlight," "Valspar Paint Program," and "Merrittt Beer Program," as well as those with his friends Kate Smith or Sophie Tucker.

"Go ahead and book me on radio," he had told Adah, "but, I don't feel like my work comes across like it should. I need to be seen, not just heard."

Ted Lewis knew that his movies that he made and his continued radio appearances during the Thirties Depression when many entertainers went broke, provided a good income. Now in the Sixties, he was still popular on an occasional radio show. The money he made from it may not have been the wealth he had in the Twenties. He knew he would never match that again, even with all the Las Vegas club work he was doing. But, radio spots, combined with movies and record royalties, plus his continuing club and theater appearances, gave him and Adah a very comfortable life. Also, the new popular medium, television, promised continued monetary rewards besides an added energy and dimension to his professional life.

Ted Lewis asked his wife to get him more television bookings on shows like Ed Sullivan's "Toast of the Town," with whom he enjoyed working. In television, he felt he had two audiences; one where it is performed live, another reaching millions of people at home who could not see his act in person. His favorite places to perform still were the clubs, and theaters in Las Vegas and other cities like Chicago, Palm Beach, and New York. Cincinnati, in his home state of Ohio, was one of his favorites and where he got some of his best reviews.

***

Ted Lewis and Eddie Cantor combine on-stage talents in their musical Review of "The Artisans" as displayed in this playbill of the production.

The Post & Times-Star
Cincinnati, Wed. August 1, 1962

Love Ted Lewis Now, Statues Come Later
BY DALE STEVENS

There is a school of performers in show business known as entertainers.

They are the stars who defy categorizing—Al Jolson, Eddie Cantor, Ted Lewis.

They also represent an era of what might be termed the good old days because they came into prominence in the roaring days.

One could become sad for a moment and think how dreadful it is going to be when the Cantors and Lewises and the Sophie Tuckers are gone, because that era will go with them.

But it would be more proper to be happy and love them while they're here. The statues can come later.

Ted Lewis came to town last night. He's at the Surf Club through Saturday, complete with battered top hat, clarinet, and the shadow.

I DON'T KNOW how many times I've seen Ted in my life. Enough that trying to review him in print again means reaching for new words that don't come easily.

Ted is of the old "roaring" school of entertainers. He struts, talks his songs, dances with the dance team, does magic along with the magician.

He makes much of his trademark, the fluttery hands. He frequently spins his hat down the arm and flips it atop his head. He never misses. He can do it while playing clarinet with the other hand, and one-handed clarinet playing is a neat trick in itself.

AT FIRST GLANCE, Ted Lewis is old-fashioned. But so is a Rolls Royce.

Look beyond the flash and you find out why Ted is a master. It's a matter of audience control.

*All the good pros have it. Ted has it in spades. His material
is honed to the point where each finger flick means something. It is
timed to what the musicians are doing, or filling in between his own
vocal phrases.*

*He tosses it in to pull attention away from the magician for a
split second (that's when the pigeon is being readied) and he even uses
whenever one of the performers is getting too many laughs.*

*At 71, he has modernized his act to include a record panto-
mime (<u>Stan Freeberg's St. George and the Dragon</u>) a quick rock-
and-roll encore for <u>Me and My Shadow</u> and a momentary "Twist."*

*And like that Rolls Royce, he still puts on that fine old show
that is his trademark.*

*At the Surf, he still has his original shadow, Eddie Chester, plus
singer Josie O'Donnell, Magician Val George and the dance team of
Manna & Mignon.*

*The small show floor is a bit confining but it does not bother
Ted. He just puts some extra oomph into his birdcalls.*

*I enjoy Ted. And the audience last night whistled and yelled
for more than he could give them. It was quite a tribute to his
showmanship and proves once again that Ted Lewis, like the Rolls
Royce, never goes out of style.*

***

There was one more thing Ted asked Adah to do.

"Georgie Jessel was talking to me about getting together
with Sophie Tucker. He thinks the three of us would be great
producing and performing in a show that brought back the old
vaudeville. Give both Georgie and Sophie a call, will you, Adah,
and ask them to dinner to talk about it. Sure, it would take a long
time to work out, but I think the three of us would be a smash."

The old soft-shoe routine.

Famed Los Angeles Times political cartoonist, Conrad, depicts 1985 Secretary of State Edwin Meese as Ted Lewis performing "Me and My Shadow," verifying the universal celebrity of Ted Lewis. Copyright Tribune Media Services. Reprinted with Permission, cartoon titled "The Old Softshoe Routine" by Conrad, published 1985.

New York, 1966

Ted Lewis and Sophie Tucker had just finished rehearsing for their upcoming extravaganza that included Georgie Jessel. Opening night was two days away.

"I think we need one more rehearsal with the band for a couple of your songs, Soph. Meet me here early tomorrow morning at nine. Okay?"

Sophie Tucker laughed her deep-down, husky-throated laugh, walked over to Ted, gave him a hug and kiss and said, "What's the matter, Teddy, haven't you heard <u>Some of These Days</u> enough? Even the ushers know the words and music by heart. She was bigger and taller than Ted, and encompassed Ted with her arms around him. "Okay, my friend, one more time can't hurt. See you tomorrow morning. Come get me in my dressing room where I'll be zonked out on the sofa from lack of sleep, thanks to you." She left the theater, mumbling to herself about "Ted Lewis, the Slave Driver," and shaking her head good-naturedly, laughing at her own joke about her long-time friend. "Love you, anyway," she called back to Ted before she went out the theater stage door.

When Ted Lewis reached Sophie Tucker's dressing room door the next morning, he knocked on the gold five-pointed star above her gilded name. Immediately he opened the door, then walked in without waiting to be invited. Sophie Tucker was dressing in the middle of the room, a white beaded dress was half-way over her head, high enough to reveal two heavy thighs that held up a pair of flesh-colored silk stockings attached to two pink garters hanging down from an enormous girdle that she wore.

"Sophie," said Ted, "have you ever thought of going on a diet?"

"Shut your damn mouth, Teddy," she said, her words muffled by the dress still on her head. She quickly pulled the rest of the dress over her body, leaving her bleached hair mussed up. She looked in the mirror and groaned. "Oh, Lord, why does this have to be a dress rehearsal? Teddy, where's your sympathy?"

"Outside this theater, my dear. You know I have none in here. When you get all those cheers from the audience, won't you be glad I was heartless?" He laughed, told her to comb her hair, and he would see her on stage. He was going to get the band ready.

Ted Lewis led the band in several minutes of playing some of their well-known pieces, until they began Some of These Days. Sophie Tucker emerged from the wing. As she walked across the stage towards the center, she smiled at applauding stagehands now sitting in several theater seats, and who were substituting for an audience. She carried a handkerchief in one hand and waved it at them. Several feather plumes stuck out from her hair. Sophie Tucker went straight to the microphone, held its post in her free hand, and began singing...

Some of these days, you're going to miss me, Honey,
Some of these days, you're going to feel so blue..."

When she finished with...

You're going to miss your big fat Mama
Some of these days,"

...she stepped back, bowed to the usher-audience, and began her dialogue routine with Ted Lewis that followed her song.

"Soph," said Ted, as he and Sophie were about to leave the theater. "Those couple of changes we made put the finishing touches on the show. It's going to be great. He kissed her cheek and said, "See you opening night, Soph."

Chapter Thirty-One

"When The Curtain Comes Down"

When Ted Lewis took his final bow in 1967 in Las Vegas at the Desert Inn, he left a legacy unique in entertainment history.

This master showman had an impact on contemporary popular music far greater than most persons have imagined. He was the first bandleader whose playing aroused in universal audiences a love for Dixie Land Jazz. Newspaper critics reported that "They went wild over his new sound when they first heard him play Jazz" at Rectors in 1916. Then, through the 1920's and 30's, as he adapted and developed his own style of jazz, his music took on a "sweeter" tone of dance and song arrangements. Pure jazz was left to special occasions and performances.

Along with other musicians, he and other bandleaders began building an "orchestral bridge" over which old time Dixie Land developed, grew, and led to new sounds, not only in jazz itself, but also its offshoots of Swing and The Big Band era.

Ted Lewis often referred to himself as the "Originator of the Big Bands," a title he gave himself for good reason. Many contemporaries–some of them who were leaders of famous Big Bands, such as Jimmy Dorsey and Benny Goodman–began their careers as members of the 1920's Ted Lewis Band. Even Paul Whiteman at one time dubbed him the "King of Jazz." In 1918,

at the age of nine, Benny Goodman imitated him on stage with his own clarinet. When these artists started their own careers as bandleaders, it was natural that the Ted Lewis style might influence each of their bands and orchestras, while their individual styles developed into musical accomplishments that took them to new heights.

Ted Lewis entertained seven United States Presidents, and performed on six continents before kings, queens, and other royalty.

Ted Lewis became the wealthiest bandleader of his day as he entertained millions during his sixty-six years of show business and sold an estimated fifty million dollars in record sales by 1955.

"I'm a showman," Ted Lewis would tell interviewers when they spoke of him as a bandleader, "and show business is my only hobby." Asked if he was going to retire, he would explain that he could never really retire because, "Being in show business is not a thing that stops. It's always there in your blood."

To the question, "Why are your shows so popular?" Lewis would reply, "My shows are always clean and entertaining. What most people want are lyrics that come straight from the heart. People want to see the same show and hear me play the way I've always played. And, if I leave out any of my familiar numbers, I get complaints."

Some critics did not appreciate the Ted Lewis brand of singing, which was more talking than singing a song. His style they described as a "sing-song croak."

These critics also considered his clarinet style "corny" and said he was a poor musician. A running joke of the day was that his clarinet experienced such pain from his playing that it pleaded, "Please, please put me back, PLEASE," and be returned to its case whenever the bandleader took it out to perform.

Ted Lewis just smiled at these criticisms and said, "This 'corn' is my bread and butter," as he continued playing his quavering renditions of When My Baby Smiles at Me, Sunny

<u>Side of the Street,</u> or <u>Alexander's Ragtime Band</u> to full houses and happy audiences. He was still pulling them in at the time of his final Broadway performance in 1965 at the Latin Quarter.

Ted Lewis, like most other bandleaders, fell victim to the new sounds and sights of music–the Rock and Roll, the Elvises, and the Beatlemanias–that brought down the Big Bands of the day because these bandleaders could not adapt their style of Swing.

In the early 1950's, there was a popular music revolution which took over the music world almost overnight. It was Rock and Roll. How music was presented, rather than how it was heard, became all-important. It became a visual medium first; audio second. Large bands dissolved and small groups took over, as the music they played was secondary to their performance. Audiences now demanded action and entertainment from these musicians and vocalists. Benign Big Band music that focused upon excellence in music was no longer popular. Most established bandleaders were not performers. They were musicians and could not make the transition. As the demand for their music ended, so did their careers.

Ted Lewis was one of the few bandleaders who survived. Unlike his contemporaries, Lewis was always the showman who performed along with his music. These factors, as well as his success in almost every other field of entertainment, enabled him to survive the shift from the jazz of Dixie Land and the Swing of the Big Bands, to the more raucous vitality of Rock and Roll artists now consuming much of the entertainment field. Although Lewis did not command the same wealth, fame, or popularity as he had prior to the 1950's, he was in demand by the Faithful who still worshiped his music and performance, was well paid, and was still a popular bandleader and entertainer. His career, unlike that of many other bandleaders, made the transition and thrived.

In 1928, Ted Lewis and his sounds and showmanship were just what Hollywood movie lords demanded. Entertainers like Al

Jolson in "The Jazz Singer" were replacing voiceless screen stars of the silent era that could not make this transition to sound. What critics heard as "sing-song croaks" and "corn" from Ted Lewis, was music to the ears of Hollywood movie moguls who saw his style as another potential for millions of silver dollars pouring into their pockets. "Come on in," they said to Ted who came willingly, equipped with battered hat and clarinet.

In the 1930's, he launched his radio career which included "Ted Lewis and His Orchestra," a series of programs featuring his band playing his numbers, along with other popular songs – We're Having a Heat Wave, That's How Rhythm Was Born, and Did You Ever See a Dream Walking? – made   famous by fellow performer and friend, Eddie Cantor. Their professional collaborations dated back to 1920 when Cantor and Lewis ap-peared in a photograph in black face with Al Jolson, on the sheet music for "O–HI–O, O–MY–O." They also appeared on the same   billing at such theaters as the grand opening for the two million dollar rebuilt Orpheum Theater in Omaha, Nebraska. They opened their own show in New York when they produced and stared in "The Artisans Present Eddie Cantor and Ted Lewis and their Combined Musical Review."

Ted Lewis was never comfortable in radio despite his success. He knew the medium was incompatible with his style, but he would continue broadcasting for many more years, still always missing his kinship with large, live audiences.

Ted Lewis was more comfortable in television and its wide audience that could see him. Combining sight and sound, television afforded him the visual exposure he sought, although live stage was always his true love.

In 1966, when Sophie Tucker collapsed on opening night before the opening curtain of the extravaganza put on by her, Ted Lewis, and George Jessel, and "The Last of the Red Hot Mamas" died shortly afterwards, the show never opened. Ted's hope of a comeback died along with his lifetime friend.

Courtesy Ted Lewis Museum, Circleville, Ohio.

In 1971, five years after Sophie Tucker died, Ted Lewis passed away in his sleep at his Central Park home in New York. The Jazz King was 81.

***

"I feel that my life hasn't been wasted and that I've done some good. I've tried to make 'Everybody Happy.' That's the finish and I can't say no more."

Ted Lewis

Book Three

Circleville
Capital of The World

Chapter Thirty-Two

"It's Three O'Clock in the Morning"

After dinner Blake and I settled down on the couch while I showed him copies I had of Ted Lewis photos from the Academy of Motion Pictures Arts and Sciences.

"You sure do look like him, especially this one," Blake said, holding up a portrait of a young Ted Lewis.

"The eyes and nose, Blake, look there," I answered as I placed my finger on the portrait and drew it across his eyes and the bridge of his nose. "Linda has that same look. But, I need glossy prints. I'll tell you my idea for the pictures after you read my notes about some of the things I found out from the Academy articles."

When he finished I said, "I found out there is a Ted Lewis Museum in Circleville, Ohio. It has his high hat and cane and clarinet, even more of his things, I suppose. Blake, I want to make a photo layout of Ted Lewis and donate it to the museum.

"They may not accept it."

" I'll just have to take that chance."

The next day I looked in every small bookstore on Hollywood Boulevard for more pictures of Ted Lewis. I finally found enough for my project.

As I drove home on a congested 405 freeway during typical Los Angeles stop-and-go after work traffic, I began to plan my photo arrangement. *The pictures aren't great. Good enough to work with, though. That one picture...I'll never forget how I felt when the salesman showed it to me. Now, if Mother just has that silhouette.* I called her when I got home.

"Mother, do you still have that small box of my school stuff?"

She evaded my question to complain about her Bridge games. Finally she said, "What did you say you wanted?"

I repeated my request. She said she knew right where my "...elementary school memorabilia is..." so I arranged to drive down the next day and get it.

After she gave me the box and I was leaving her house, Joe handed me an old Sees candy tin and said, "Here's some of my sugarless, butterless, low calorie fudge for you to take home to Blake. I know how much you two like it."

I thanked him, kissed them both, and drove home, laughing every time I thought of the look of pain I would see on Blake's face when I handed him "Joe's Favorite Fudge."

The first thing I did when I arrived home was to place the box Mother gave me on the bed, open it, and search through old school papers of mine. There was a painting or two, a poem - *Oh Joshua tree, so straight and tall* - ribbons, and a clay imprint of a small hand: mine.

I found the silhouette on the bottom of the box. Gently, I placed it on the bed. *Be careful. It's almost fifty years old and might tear.* I backed away a few steps, my eyes still glued to this new-found treasure. Then I retrieved the photo of Ted Lewis from my dresser drawer and placed his picture on the bed beside the silhouette. Now, lying side-by-side, was a full-length photograph in full black profile of Ted Lewis as his famous Shadow, and lying next to it was a silhouette, full head profile also in black, of a six-year-old girl with long corkscrew curls. As I saw the contours of one facial profile blend into an almost exact replica of the contours of the other facial profile, I let my finger trace along

Silhouette of Ted Lewis, "The Jazz King"

Silhouette of Dawn Whipple as a child

the lines and curves of each face. I allowed my hand to follow over each forehead, down the nose, across the lips, and end after it pursued the shape of both slightly receding chins. *Not my best feature, but I wouldn't change it now for the world.*

The silhouette had been one of those handmade-at-school Christmas gifts elementary grade children make for their parents. I remembered how long we first graders stood in line for our turns to have a teacher draw each profile on a page of large white paper hanging on an easel. When I returned to my classroom with mine, I traced around it on a piece of black poster paper, cut around the profile, then pasted it on to white poster paper. I was so proud when my mother opened my Christmas gift and found a black silhouette portrait of her only child. It was one of the few school mementos of mine that Mother kept, and I wondered if she, too, had recognized the resemblance when she opened my gift?

I would now return it to a box where, accompanied by the Ted Lewis photo, the two images would remain together, a silent testimony to what might have been.

Chapter Thirty-Three

"Homemade Sunshine"

When finished, my Ted Lewis photo layout measured approximately two and one-half by four feet and was surrounded by a gilded frame.

"Do you think they'll accept this?" Blake asked when I showed it to him.

"Possibly not," I said. "I guess we wait and see. "Blake, I've decided I'm going to write that Ted Lewis biography we've never found. Ted Lewis and what he did for music and entertainment will be completely lost to the world if someone doesn't record his life and his accomplishments. I want to be the one who writes it."

When the letter came in the mail a few weeks later, I was so excited I could hardly open it. The letterhead read:

Ted Lewis Museum
OF CIRCLEVILLE AND PICKAWAY COUNTY
P.O. Box 492
Circleville, Ohio 43113

March 11, 1984

Did they accept my picture or not? Read it and find out.

Ted Lewis Museum receives photolayout gift from California writer. Permission of The Circleville Herald.

"Soon it will be a month since I received the fabulous picture of Ted Lewis Movie Stills for the Ted Lewis Museum. Please, forgive me for not writing to you sooner..."

I stopped reading the letter, looked in the envelope, and took out a piece of folded newspaper. It was an article from the Circleville Herald illustrated by a photograph of two men who were holding for display my picture layout of Ted Lewis. Under the newspaper photo was the caption: **"New at the Museum"** and it read; "Judge William Ammer (left), president of the Ted Lewis Museum board and board member Ben Gordon display the Lewis photographs recently presented to the museum by a California writer." *They accepted it.*

I raced to read the headline underneath the picture caption: **Ted Lewis Museum receives photographs**, and the article that followed. "Circleville's Ted Lewis Museum has been presented with a new series of photographs of the famous song and dance man for which the museum is named. Dawn Williams...who is doing research on Lewis, gave the photographs...." The remainder of the article gave a brief summary of my background and purpose in donating the picture. The remainder of letter confirmed the newspaper article with..."It is absolutely a masterpiece and I want everybody to know it is at the museum..." and ended with"...grateful appreciation for this outstanding addition to our Ted Lewis Museum." The letter was signed by the museum Coordinator.

I wonder if she saw the passport picture of me that I glued on the back of the picture?

Chapter Thirty-Four

"My Old Flame"

The tape recorder lay hidden beside me on the black leather seat of my seat of my white T-Bird. "She'll never see it," I said out loud to myself as I approached Mother's home in Carlsbad. I had covered it with my red sweater, leaving its speaker exposed. *Maybe I should be a sleuth.*

My reason for the camouflaged tape recorder? Except for brief telephone conversations, this was the first time Joe had allowed my mother and me to be alone since she told me the truth about Ted Lewis. Today I was taking her to lunch in La Jolla, an upscale beach city a few miles north of San Diego. During our half-hour drive each way, I planned to ask my mother questions about him and wanted to preserve her answers on tape. If she knew of the recorder, I was afraid she would be self-conscious and it would affect her answers. I wanted her to respond truthfully and with no inhibitions.

As I listened to the tape the next day, I regretted that I'd had to record my mother's reminiscence while driving. The engine sounds almost overwhelmed her voice in many places. Despite this interference, I was able to transcribe her answers and record them in a notebook I called:

My Mother and Ted Lewis

*I have to start my story when I met and married Fred
Whipple, the man who would introduce me to Ted Lewis.*

*I had just moved back to L.A after touring in an act with
Colonel Diamond, an eighty year old dancer, in his act called, "Youth
and Old Age." I was supposed to be his granddaughter and dance
partner on stage. In Los Angeles I got a job at a movie studio as an
extra and dancer. During the filming of a movie, I met another extra,
Barbara. We decided to go matinee dancing, and were to meet at
the Alexandria Hotel in Los Angeles. When I arrived, Barbara was
already talking to two older men. One was Charles Baad, manager of
the hotel, and the other was Fred Whipple.*

*Well, to make a long story short, Fred said he dearly loved
dancing and invited Barbara and me to go dinner dancing at the
famous "Indian Room" where Paul Whiteman and his band were
playing. Fred Knew Paul Whiteman, and he sat with us between
dances. Jack Dempsey, the prizefighter, and his wife were also there,
so we met them, too. While we were dancing, Fred invited me to see
a play the next night. Oh, what a joyous afternoon. You can imagine
how I felt when I saw a limo with Fred in it arrive to pick me up.
I was staying with Mama and Papa, so I introduced them to Fred.
Before we left their house, he invited them to have dinner with us a
couple of nights later.*

*When he took us home, he asked me if I would write to him
in Detroit while he was there on business. Of course, I said, "yes."
He was so intelligent and interesting...and distinguished looking. We
exchanged only a few letters before he asked me to marry him,*

*My parents agreed, and he sent me a nice big check for expenses.
Then off I went to marry him in Detroit. Even though he was
thirty-six years older than me, I was thrilled to be marrying such a
wonderful person. What a man!*

Dawn, this is where Ted Lewis comes in. Fred's work, as you

My mother, Ruth Dean Whipple with Fred Whipple enjoying their Chicago trip on March 4, 1923.

know, was establishing studies for colleges and took him all over the United States. Since we had no children, I always went with him. Well, Fred and the Lewises were friends, so we saw his show if we were in a nearby town. I was thrilled when this occurred because we usually went dinner dancing with them at some all-night supper club after his show. He was so charming, as was his wife, Adah.

I remember one of these times in San Francisco. Ted and I somehow managed to go out alone to Purcell's, a Barbary Coast nightclub. Guess what? He introduced me to everyone as "Mrs. Lewis." Of course I was thrilled and enjoyed every minute of it.

On the way back to the St, Francis Hotel, where we were all staying, we did some mild petting, but nothing immoral (so to speak, Dawn). You can imagine that both Adah and Fred were very mad, and who can blame them? Adah was just furious with Ted, though not so mad that we didn't all go out the next night after Ted's show to the Tecaux Tavern where we met Ted's father.

Over the next several years there were many similar meetings when the four of us would go night clubbing after Ted's evening show. One particular time in Boston at the Pemberton Inn was similar to many of these meetings we had. The four of us were having dinner when Ted told the Maitre-De Hotel, in private, that I was Virginia Vallé, a popular Hollywood star. Fred, he said, was my manager and described Fred and me as marvelous dancers and close friends of his. Ted announced we would perform an exhibition dance. Well, Fred and I were shocked, but agreed to dance. We were the hit of the evening.

It was six years, Dawn, between my first meeting with Ted and our love affair in Los Angeles when you were conceived. Ted came to Hollywood in June 1928, to start a film career. At the same time he was also playing at the Palace Theater in Los Angeles.

While Fred was away on business, he wrote to me that I should go to see Ted's show, then get together afterwards with Ted and Adah. I did go by myself, but Adah was not there and Ted was alone. Ted seemed thrilled to see me. After I watched his act from the theater wings, I went with him back to his dressing room. After a few hugs and kisses, he asked me to meet him at the Ambassador after his show. I said, "Yes," knowing what would naturally occur. Ted said the theater manager had loaned him his apartment for the night and Ted gave me the room number.

When I arrived at the apartment, Ted met me at the door and led me inside, kissed me and said, "I've been waiting six years for this." What happened next, of course, was the "bedroom scene."

Getting pregnant never occurred to me. I had been married to Fred all those years and it never happened. I thought I was immune. But, after missing a couple of periods while Fred was still away, I knew I was going to have a baby.

How was I going to break this news to Fred?

A few weeks later Fred called from San Francisco and told me to drive up and meet him. I knew I had to tell him, although I was not showing much. Our first night at dinner I was so scared. Fred asked me if I had seen Ted and Adah in L.A? My answer was to tell him the awful truth: I was pregnant and was going to have Ted's baby. He turned chalk white and hardly spoke the rest of the evening, except to tell me I had to have an abortion. I told him I absolutely refused. I was going to have this baby.

That night I didn't sleep. I don't think Fred did either. By the next morning, after thinking things over, Fred said that he was responsible for what happened. He said "I should never have told you to go see Ted alone." Then he took me in his arms and said, "We'll have the baby as yours and mine."

I was so relieved. I wanted you so badly. His acceptance of my pregnancy and willingness to raise you as his own made me so happy. Driving all the way home from San Francisco to our apartment on Kingsley Drive in Hollywood, my heart soared. And in a few days I went with him on the remainder of his trip as he fulfilled contracts that he had with more colleges.

Then you were born and most of the rest you know. Fred died when you were three and left me penniless. I had to put you in an orphanage till I could support you. Then, remember how I told you that someone wanted to adopt you after Fred died, but I wouldn't hear of it? I never told you who it was, and you never asked. Dawn, it was Ted Lewis who wanted to raise you as his adopted daughter. The problem was, Adah wouldn't hear of it, either. And who can blame her? She didn't want some other woman's child.

Did I ever see Ted again? Yes. Once. He was playing at the Paramount Theater in Los Angeles, so Charlotta and I went to see him. Just before his show started I went back stage. He just had a minute before he went on, and asked me how I was. Then he said, "When are you going to get Dawn out of that orphanage?" I'll never forget how sad he looked."

Dawn, there's one thing I've always regretted not telling you. Remember the time we went to see Ted Lewis at the Orpheum and your grandmother stayed home? It was the time I wouldn't let you go up on stage when Ted asked the children in the audience to come up? Well, I'd given a note to an usher to take back to Ted telling him that Dawn and I were in the audience. I also asked him to sing <u>When My Baby Smiles at Me</u> for us. I was just too scared to have you meet him, and what he might say. I'm sorry, Dawn, I should have let you go up on the stage and meet the man who was your real father.

***

About six months after my mother told Fred Whipple that she was pregnant, a news item appeared in the March 8, 1929 issue of the Hollywood Daily Citizen:

DAUGHTER BORN: Mr. and Mrs. Fred Herbert Whipple of 1825 North Kingsley Drive are happy over the birth of a little seven-pound daughter, born at home yesterday. The little girl was born early in the morning, and is named Dawn Whipple.

Chapter Thirty-Five

"Farewell Blues"

Who would ever think that the United States Secret Service had to protect Jesse Jackson and Caesar Chavez from me?

In 1985 Blake and I had moved to McFarland, California, a San Joaquin Valley speck of farmland twenty-five miles north of Bakersfield. The Depression Era's famed Highway 99 dissects half of the town's acreage. "Population 6,217" boasts a sign for travelers headed towards either San Francisco or Los Angeles. Only those who live in this tiny town are reminded daily of how many of its eighty-five per cent migrant workers live here. To a stranger looking at its boarded up storefronts, vacant sidewalks, and silent streets, McFarland looks like a ghost town, and the sign seems a ridiculous exaggeration.

Is this as good as it gets? Yes, I finally concluded after a couple of years trying to adjust to my forced and unwanted retirement, a term I always hated.

Keeping busy was my immediate solution for survival. For a year I taught Speech at California State University Bakersfield. In Delano, six miles north of McFarland, I was hired as a photographer and reporter on The Delano Record. I loved both jobs and found Mcfarland full of energetic and intelligent people. To this city girl, however, rural McFarland seemed overlooked by civilization. My oldest son's words as I left my Seal Beach home, along with any hope of going to Circleville and working on my Ted Lewis biography, kept coming back to me. "Mom," Dana said, "people don't move to McFarland, they move from it."

During the same time that I arrived in McFarland, a cancer scare involving pesticides and contaminated water threw local migrant workers into a panic because some of their children simultaneously became afflicted with the disease. While taking pictures at a local protest rally attended by Jackson, Chavez, and hundreds of other sympathizers wishing to aid the victims, two Secret Service agents thought I was photographing too close to these famous activists. After shouting at me to stop taking pictures and move farther away from the two men, they escorted me to a safe distance away from the celebrities they were protecting. I can imagine a possible National Inquirer headline now:

JACKSON AND CHAVEZ SAVED BY SECRET SERVICE FROM CRAZED MCFARLAND HOUSEWIFE AND 'DEATH BY NIKON.'

Blake and I began to have serious marital problems even before we moved to the valley town. His desire to sell our business, home and retire ten years before we had planned, then to leave what he considered a choking metropolitan existence for the solitude offered by McFarland's isolated remoteness, and to live almost 150 miles distance from our grown children, proved to be heaven-on-earth for him, but hell for me. After living there almost two years, our problems escalated until I finally knew I had to leave.

Piling clothes into my T-Bird, barely able see out the back window, and mourning my dead marriage, I left McFarland for Motel Six in Long Beach.

At Bakersfield, I stopped for gas. The attendant could have been John Wayne ambling up to my open window. He poked his head into my T-Bird, and looked at the mess in the back seat.

"M'am, fill 'er up?"

"Please," I said.

After filling the gas tank and checking the oil, he sauntered back to take my credit card. Quizzically, he stood there a few moments, and again assessed my car's back seat with its overflow.

"M'am," he finally said, "pardon me for askin,' but you're the third lady to come in here in the past two hours, cryin' and with a back seat chock full o' stuff. M'am, kin ya please tell me where ya'all are goin'?

"Probably through Hell," I answered. I pulled away from the station and back onto Old 99 to begin my journey southward as a single woman.

I'm just a Bag Lady in a T-Bird.

Chapter Thirty-Six

"Home Town"

The Ted Lewis Museum in Circleville, Ohio, displays this High Hatted Tragedian of Song's memorabilia inside a building that is squeezed by two others on either side until it is shaped like a piece of apple pie. Its storefront window seems normal enough, with one large pane of glass at the side of a single door, the entrance for this dedication to the Jazz King, his life and accomplishments. Piped from inside the museum to the outside sidewalk and street so that pedestrians may hear them, are familiar Ted Lewis songs.

As visitors enter the front door and walk through the museum from front to back, a marked narrowing of the room occurs, until only a tiny space remains that allows a slim back door exit. The reason for this "piece of pie" shape? History credits the Hopewell culture of prehistoric Indians, who lived in Ohio from 900 to 1100, for the original circle shape of the city. In the early eighteen hundreds, the town's redevelopment was planned so as to retain the form of a circle, with streets radiating from a center point marked by an octagonal brick courthouse.

Citizens eventually became dissatisfied with the town's pie shape. On March 23, 1838 the first steps were taken to square off Circleville. After many years of living as "round town," the town then squared its circle shape, a feat considered impossible in geometry.

One building, now shared with the Ted Lewis Museum, would be exempt and remain a triangle. Why? Perhaps in this circle-to-rectangle metamorphose, one small spot had to retain its original shape in order to enable the rest of town to fit.

It was 1991 when I first saw this permanent reminder of Circleville's Indian heritage and the unique site chosen to house the museum that was dedicated to the life of Ted Lewis, "Ohio's Favorite Son."

***

When I called the Museum, I spoke to the Coordinator and told her I was writing a biography of Ted Lewis and wanted to do research at the museum. We agreed on the April date that I would make my first visit to Circleville, and she offered to pick me up at the airport in Columbus. Her assistant would be with her.

"How will I know you when I arrive?" I said. I was excited about my trip and wanted every detail assured. She said she would surprise me.

As I left the airplane and walked into the waiting area at Port Columbus International Airport, I saw my surprise in front of me. Waving high above the heads of other deplaning passengers were two identical photographs of Ted Lewis. Two women were each holding up one of the pictures high in the air and waving it back and forth.

They seemed to be looking for someone in the crowd. I rushed towards the two ladies, we exchanged greetings, then we left the airport in Columbus and headed to Circleville. Near the end of the drive and off to the right of the road, a small sign appeared with "Ted Lewis Museum" printed in large letters. We stopped just long enough for me to take a picture of it. We arrived in the tiny city only a short jaunt later.

Circleville, Ohio, I thought, is Norman Rockwell country,

an artist's model for his mid-America paintings of Hometown, USA during the nineteen hundreds. The town was now sheltered under a pale light of evening's shade, and a muted daylight with its soft pink undertones fell on its homes, stores, and a striped barber shop pole.

"It's too late to see the museum," the Coordinator said as she drove by it, "but, we'll see it tomorrow. It's close to the Guest House where you're staying. That way you can walk to the museum when you do your research. Oh, be sure to have breakfast over there." She pointed to a small restaurant with a sign that read "Henn House" in large letters. "The owner is Ruth Henn. Tell her I told you to eat there."

Early the next morning, after I introduced myself to Ruth Henn, I explained that I was doing research at the museum. She sat me at one of the small tables for two that lined one wall of the tiny restaurant. Two picnic type tables with chairs on each side covered most of the remaining area, leaving a small passage that extended from the kitchen to the front door. Several people were already eating at the large tables. I was the only person occupying a small one.

"Here's the menu, dear. Coffee?" Ruth Henn was a small, pleasant woman with snow-white hair. She added, "Welcome to Circleville and the Henn House."

"Black coffee please. And just bring me two eggs scrambled, with grapefruit juice, small."

While I ate, several persons came in and joined those already seated at the large tables, greeting them as if they were family. Each one occasionally glanced at me. Some smiled as they caught my eye. I smiled back and nodded. Other customers seemed more stern and cautious, as if assessing this newcomer in town. It was the first time I ever had breakfast with Middle America.

A message was waiting for me when I returned to my room. The Coordinator wanted to show me some things before opening the Museum, and would pick me up in her car.

One of these was the home where Benjamin and Pauline Friedman raised their five sons: Theodore, Max, Leon, Milton, and Edgar. It resembled pictures I had seen of mid-west homes.

"Maybe we can go in later," she said, "but first I have some place very special to take you." Then she handed me a crimson rosebud, told me to hold it, and she would explain more when we arrived at our destination just a few miles outside of town. "Glad you brought your camera. You'll need it."

We drove under a gray, over cast April sky that covered homes set on large plots of land. A few hid an occasional bit of snow leftover under surrounding bushes or other shelters from the sun.

After several miles, she turned the car and drove under an arch that read on top, "Forest Cemetery." We arrived at a large gravesite with tall, white markers etched with various Friedman family names and stopped at this family plot. One marker bore an impression of a high hat and cane. The name on it was "Theodore Leopold Friedman."

"This is the Friedman family plot," she said. "I thought you'd like to put a rose on Ted's grave." She picked up my camera. "Show me how this works and I'll take a picture."

I was first to break the silence as we drove back to town." That's a moment I'll never forget," I said.

Arriving at the museum, she let me out of the car in front of the building.

"Wait here. I'm going to park in the back. I'll come through the building and open the front door."

After a few minutes of waiting, music outside the museum started playing. I could hear Ted Lewis singing, <u>Me and My Shadow</u>.

During our ride back from the cemetery, the Coordinator had given me both the historical and physical background of Circleville and the museum. She suggested I go through the building the same as any other visitor, from front to back, but that I might prefer being on my own rather than her acting as guide during my first visit. I agreed.

"But, I would appreciate the 'guided tour' later," I said.

As I approached the front door, the light went on and illuminated the inside of the museum. When I looked through the window, I saw a glass case centered in the middle of the room. It displayed two items that I had not seen since I was a young girl. They were the same battered high hat and clarinet that were a part of Ted Lewis and his act as he entertained audiences throughout the world. *This is as close to my father that I'll ever feel as long as I'm in this world.*

Through the window, I could see my hostess, who was now walking towards the front door, unlock and open it, then hold it wide for me to enter. I walked through the entrance, and went directly to the glass case, protector of treasures that belonged to Ted Lewis, now displayed for the world to see.

As I stood in front of the display, looking at its contents I thought of the many times I saw him wearing this same top hat and playing this same clarinet. *How I wish I had known him.* In front of me was the cane that twirled during hundreds of <u>Me and My Shadow</u> routines. A piece of sheet music, one of his many famous songs, lay between them.

Standing there alone, I wondered how often Ted Lewis had asked his audience, "Is everybody happy?" How I wanted him to hear me reply, "Yes," just as I did so many years ago when I was part of that audience. Now, being here in Circleville at the Ted Lewis Museum, looking at these icons that distinguished him as an entertainer beloved throughout the world, I felt so close to this man I now knew as my father, that it was almost as if he were saying to me, "Welcome home, Dawn."

Me and My Father's Shadow

Afterward

"Tiger Rag"

Both Ted Lewis and Lou Walters, famed entertainment impresario, owner of the Latin Quarter nightclubs where the Jazz King often performed, were members of the Friars Club that was established in 1904 as one of the world's most prestigious entertainment organizations. For almost a century, with its celebrity roasts, testimonial dinners, and Friars Frolics, the Friars Club has been a leading force in entertainment.

At the Ted Lewis Museum in Circleville, Ohio, and The Academy of Motion Picture Arts and Sciences, my research uncovered scrapbooks, papers, letters, and press clippings preserved as a record and tribute to the famed showman's life and career, including the following article. This, I thought, best describes what Ted Lewis was all about, and his impact on the world of entertainment. It was published in the <u>Las Vegas Review-Journal</u> of Thursday, May 24, 1962, and appeared in the column, "Behind the Footlights" by Lou Walters. His article was entitled, "Ted Lewis: A Veteran showman's Candid Appraisal of a Veteran Performer:"

"Later that evening at the Friars Club the talk got around to (George) Jessel and the wonderful emceeing he did at this banquet, and the hundreds of others where he presides for worthy as well as selfish purposes, to such an extent as to cause him to be called, America's Mr. Toastmaster.

NATURALLY THE discussion took a turn as to who might be considered the greatest emcee of today and the past generations.

<u>My vote went to Ted Lewis</u>, and for once every Friar agreed. Why, Ted Lewis?

BECAUSE THIS bandy legged, high hatted tragedian of Jazz can make any ordinary act look good, any good act look better, and any great act appear wonderful.

I've never heard Ted say that the next act is "the greatest." I've never heard him ask any act to "come back, they love you, take another bow."

His is a more subtle method. He'll stay in the background waving his hands as he directs the orchestra in back of him, only interjecting his own personality where it will enhance the actor's turn. I've seen him take ordinary little girls, give them something to do with him, and make them look like stars. Away from him they are almost nothing, and with him they are sensational.

THE MOST ORDINARY act, through some kind of magic, projects. Artists who get roars of laughter, hysterical applause while they are with him, fade out into mediocrity when they leave him.

I'll be double deuced if I know what it is. The hour show he presents is an hour of pure personality, without him 'twould well be a bore.

So my vote goes for Ted, long may his black cane and battered hat twirl at his fingertips, may his "shadow" grow longer as long as there is a clarinet to play or an audience to listen."

Acknowledgements

I envy those writers of non-fiction who can fill up their "thank you" page, such as the following acknowledgement text, with pages of names, institutions etc. for the help given to them in writing their books. Though mine is brief, it could be longer if I were to detail how important each of these persons is for contributing to the begininning, middle, and end of Me and My Fathr's Shadow - A Daughter's Quest and Biography of Ted Lewis "The Jazz King."

These accolades go to the following: The Academy of Motion Pictures Arts and Sciences Margarita Herrick Library in Hollywood, California, where so much of movie industry memorabilia is methodically housed, and to all of its wonderful staff, so generous with their time, information, and smiles; to the Ted Lewis Museum in Circleville, Ohio, and those there whose help and guidance was indispensable, and truly made their city "The Capital of the World;" to the professor who told me, "You must write a book," and many years later guided me when my writing was going in both the wrong or the right direction; to all my many friends who so graciously supported me in this quest; to my computer technician, John Green, whose expertise solved my computer problems; to my wonderful Publicist, Milton Kahn, to my talented Production Manager, Scott Willis; to **The Exotic**

World Burlesque Museum in Helendale, California; especially to that wonderful lady, Sara Weintraub, who spent so many hours with me in her Palm Desert home sharing with me her reminiscenses of Ted and Adah Lewis; and to those who maintain the many websites that depict the entertainment world of the 1900's....

Dawn Williams

Epilogue

"THAT OLD HIGH HAT OF MINE"

Is Everybody Happy?

THAT OLD HIGH HAT OF MINE

Well, it's a hat that has a history -- tho of old and
    quaint design --
No hat was e'er held higher than this old high hat of
    mine.
It has walked -- *walked* with Booth and Barrett
It bowed to Sarah Bernhardt too.
It has taken strolls with those gentle souls, Nat
    Goodwin, and John Drew
And it's hung in that Diamond Horseshoe just to hear
    Caruso sing.
Why it stood in line at Shakespeare's shrine --
It has raised -- to the praise -- of a king.
And it played -- it played ten twenty thirty --
It walked the ties all day --
Since 1906 it played the sticks, from Maine to
    Mandalay.
It has ballyhooed a tent show. *Ah* I know it's old --
    but it's not to blame.
I was given it by an old legit -- *Say* you'd start if you
    heard his name.
He said, "Son -- take it -- I'm washed up -- but *that*
    old high hat isn't through"
It loves to play -- and some day -- who knows -- it
    may become a part of you.
And somehow I know it's happy -- tho it hasn't shape
    or shine --
But it thrills me so -- just to have you know -- this old
    high hat of mine....*Ted Lewis*

Me and My Father's Shadow

Bibliography

Alcoate, John W., *Talking Films - NO.1, Film Daily Yearbook.* New York: John W. Alcoate, 1929.

Barrios, Richard. *A Song In The Dark.* New York: Oxford University Press, Inc., 1995.

Berle, Milton. *An Autobiography With Haskel Frankel.* New York: Delacorte Press, 1974.

Berle, Milton. *My Father's Uncle Miltie With Brad Lewis.* New York: Barricade Books, Inc., 1999.

Burk, Margaret Tante. *Are The Stars Out Tonight?* Los Angeles: Round Table West Ambassador Hotel, 1980.

Burke, Billie. *With A Feather On My Nose.* New York: Appleton-Century-Cross, Inc., 1949.

Burns, George. *All My Best Friends.* New York: G.P. Putnam's Sons, 1989.

Burns, George. *Gracie.* New York: The Penguin Group, 1988.

Cantor, Eddie. *As I Remember Them.* New York: Van Rees Press, 1963.

Cantor, Eddie. *My Life Is In Your Hands* and *Take My Life.* Two Autobiographies of Eddie Cantor. New York: Cooper Square Press, 2000.

Christiansen, Dick. *Ted Lewises Reflect Felicity of Forty-Five Years.* Los Angeles Mirror-News, May 7, 1960.

Firestone, Ross. *Swing Swing Swing.* New York: W.W. Norton & Company, 1993.

Lamparski, Richard. *Whatever Became Of...Vol. II.* New York: Ace Star Book, 1970.

Megill, Donald D./Demory, Richard S. *Englewood Cliffs.* New York: Prentice-Hall, Inc., 1984.

Othman, Fredrick C., *Lewis Hopes For Happier Movie Stint.* Hollywood: Hollywood Citizen. May 29, 1941.

Rogers, Ginger. *Ginger My Story.* New York: Harper Collins Publishers, 1991.

Sheridan, Phil. *Those Wonderful Old Downtown Theaters.* Columbus: Phil Sheridan, 1978.

Sheridan, Phil. *Those Wonderful Old Downtown Theaters, Vol. II.* Columbus: Phil Sheridan, 1984.

Sheridan, Phil. *Those Wonderful Old Downtown Theaters, Vol. III.* Columbus: Phil Sheridan, 1992.

Simon, George T. *The Big Bands.* New York: Macmillan Publsihing Co., 1967.

Stearns, Marshall. *The Story of Jazz.* New York: Mentor Books; The New American Library of World Literature, Inc., 1958.

Walker, Leo. *The Big Band Almanac Revised Edition.* New York: Da Capo Press, 1978.

Williams, Jett with Pamela Thomas. *Ain't Nothin' As Sweet As My Baby.* New York: 1990.

Williams, Martin. *The Jazz Tradition, new and revised edition.* New York: Oxford University Press, 1983.

Wilson, John S. *The Collector's Jazz Traditional and Swing.* New York: J.B. Lippincott Company, 1958.

Fund Raising For Memorial Slows Down, New York Times, Dec. 9 1975.

Police Hold Throng at "Show of Shows," Vol.1, 1913-1931. November 21, 1929.

Ted Lewis, Motion Picture Almanac, 1930.

Unemployed Ted Lewis Seeks Job, Los Angeles Herald-Examiner, Dec. 12, 1970.